For Bot,
my girl Friday and devoted wife,
and for Angelica and Marie
who inspired me to write this autobiography.

Generative AI was not used in the drafting, editing, design, or production of this book. 100% author-created content.

Author: TJ Hawk
Edition: 2
Date Published: May 2021
Publisher: Terry Mallon
Cover design: Graphics layout by Terry Mallon.

© 2021 GreyHawk Aviation LLC. All rights reserved. This material may not be reproduced, displayed, modified, or distributed without the prior and express written permission of the copyright holder. All inquiries via GreyHawk@1sos.com

Books by TJ Hawk

Gar Randolph Series

The Ghost of Siam

Sungtan's Gold

Salvaged

Papua

Kolovalu's Revenge

Historical Fiction

Brothers of Fortune, A Story of the Philippines

Autobiography

Walk Run Fly

Chapter 1

You only live once, but if you do it right, once is enough.
– Mae West

ENJOY LIFE. SMILE. LAUGH MORE. FOCUS ON the important stuff and lighten up on the rest. Life's a daring adventure if you're willing to hold on tight. That's been my life in a nutshell.

Yesterday, I gazed toward Mt Fuji's breathtaking majesty in a reflective mood.

How did a simple Wisconsin boy like me find his way around the world to this point in time?

Mine has been a journey of close family ties, of spiritual and personal growth. I reshaped foolishness into discipline, developed character, found relationships, and made commitments.

Major milestones occurred along the way and professional maturity became one of them. It started once I became a pilot where I found myself immersed in an environment espousing core values of integrity and excellence. Doing the minimum lacked satisfaction. I wanted to do more. As a staff officer, I spread my wings and discovered greater potential. As a leader, I found compassion and empathy vastly more rewarding than power and control.

Mentorship came at odd times. A seventy-year-old helicopter pilot showed me the joy of flight as we watched hawks glide along rising updrafts. A gifted priest brought religious beliefs down to earth in a way that tied them to my everyday actions. An ex-prisoner of war instructor pilot demanded excellence with a tough, yet gentle approach, often when flying upside down, tucked between three other jets, and approaching the sound barrier. In the end, I became a composite of all those who touched my life.

Circumstance adds an unexpected dimension to everyone's life. Some people win the lottery, others struggle against disease. I seemed to find the unexpected while flying aircraft, from a gearbox-draining oil leak over Korea to mechanical failures in all the wrong places. I crashed and waited for a flash fire to engulf me. Another time I thought I died. Thank goodness I'd gotten it wrong.

It seems I became a magnet for natural disasters as well. From flying search and rescue missions to refueling helicopters in remote locations to setting up mission planning operations, I got close to the victims. In the case of Mt. Pinatubo's volcanic eruption, I found myself as one of them.

These things all seemed natural enough at the time, except for Mt. Pinatubo which definitely felt exceptional. They did, however, impact my view of the world. I enjoy life. I smile at others. There's laughter in our family. I've found that most things aren't worth worrying about and that many people suffer more than I imagine.

To the best of my recollection, this is how it all happened …

"Grab Terry!"

Mom's panicked voice pierced the air as the cold Atlantic undercurrent pulled me down. It's surprising that I still love swimming in lakes and oceans. I weighed in at two years old, too young to know fear or caution. Uncle Tom, a gentle giant who'd spent much of his life around Chicago inspecting grain-hauling ships, charged into Topsail's crashing surf, snatched me from the strong North Carolina undercurrent and pulled me to safety.

We existed as a military family back then. Dad served as a Marine Corps artillery officer during World War II and later commanded a reserve detachment in Green Bay, Wisconsin. He assaulted Guadalcanal in the Solomon Islands and shelled Naha in Okinawa before returning home to Chicago. When opportunity pointed him north toward Green Bay, Dad joined forces with a business partner and formed an accounting firm.

The Korean War uprooted our short-lived stationary existence. We became beachcombers walking the sandy shores along North Caroline's Topsail Island, then explored El Paso's cactus-infested hillsides, and ultimately migrated back to Green Bay. From as early as I can remember, Mom, Dad, Uncle Tom O'Brien, and my older sister, Kathy, comprised our family unit. My brother, Greg, came into the picture in Green Bay four years after me.

A '52 Kaiser Allstate automobile transported us from military base to military base. It fell short of being the Cadillac of the day, but it appeared oddly stylish and functional. Henry Kaiser and Joseph Frazer incorporated the Kaiser-Frazer Company to compete against the Big Three – GM, Ford, and Chrysler. Their upstart company epitomized the American spirit, producing a fiberglass-bodied sports car called the Kaiser-Darrin-Frazer 161.

It's said that a man's car defines his essence. Dad fashioned himself to be rather conservative but at his core, he harbored a surprisingly adventurous spirit. In many ways, this car reflected it. In the years ahead, that same out-of-the-box essence found a warm embrace in our household.

As much as we loved the car, we experienced its dark side one afternoon. A moderately sharp bend in the road caused the rear passenger door to unexpectedly swing open. I rolled unceremoniously across the seat toward the opening when Mom reached around and latched onto the scruff of my neck. Cars didn't have seatbelts back then. Oddly, my brush with disaster never fazed me. I'd been either too young or too naive to know how quickly calamity could strike.

Chapter 2

You have brains in your head. You have feet in your shoes. You can steer yourself in any direction you choose.
You're on your own. And you know what you know. And YOU are the one who'll decide where to go…
– Dr. Seuss, Oh the Places You'll Go

OUR HOUSE AT 1221 OREGON STREET MARKED the center of my universe. My four-year-old world stretched for eight houses to either side. I slipped under the backyard fence when adventurous juices flowed and cautiously explored the mysterious unknowns of the adjoining block. These bold explorations ended when a polio outbreak struck Green Bay. Mom chatted in fearful tones with neighboring wives. Rumors of a stricken child put everyone on edge. A polio vaccine wouldn't be available for weeks.

Nurses eventually inoculated us. Parents eased restrictions and over time freed us to again traipse about our Oregon Street kingdom.

With polio in the rear-view mirror, I found an opportunity to acquaint myself with gravity … as in falling from a high enough perch to accelerate before abruptly coming to a stop.

One of our favorite nearby places, Murphy Park, featured giant pine trees, picnic tables, swings, and monkey bars. Trees diffused the hot afternoon sunshine while adding a refreshing fragrance. An ever-present slow-moving breeze always cooled the park. Picnic tables rested on a carpet of pine needles, and the fifteen-foot-tall monkey bars begged to be climbed.

Back in the 1950s, monkey bars looked significantly different than today. Imagine a giant drinking glass, an inverted tumbler made of a broad open mesh. Murphy Park's monkey bars consisted of two-inch steel tubing. In today's world, they'd be considered downright dangerous, but for me, they represented challenge and adventure.

I soon conquered the height and became the king of my world. Then my grip slipped. I awoke a minute later in my mother's arms. The knot on my forehead served as a lasting reminder to hold on tighter.

That same year my brother and I shared a bunk bed. The top bunk became mine based on age. One night I dreamed of flying, of feeling free. I hit the floor, confused. Dad replaced the wooden safety railing and I eventually went back to sleep no worse for the wear.

Saturdays never came soon enough. During the summer months, my mom issued ten movie tickets to my sister, brother, and me. We carefully detached the weekly ticket from its perforated sheet. That tiny piece of stiff paper felt like gold in our hands and it granted us entry into the movie theater. The movies generally featured Westerns. However, we anticipated each viewing with pure childish excitement regardless of the genre. Neighborhood moms took turns dropping us off at the theater around 10 a.m. and later fetched us at noon. Occasionally we'd watch the movie twice and ride home at 3 p.m.

We owned a single telephone, a modern one that hung on the wall and sported a rotary dial. It seldom rang. Long-distance calls seemed impractical and expensive. Nonetheless, something as simple as a wall phone convinced us all that we'd joined the modern age of technology. In 1956, my dad purchased a black and white television.

We watched it once a week, on Saturday night after taking baths. When Uncle Tom babysat, he spread a thick blanket across the kitchen table. My brother, sister, and I laid on our stomachs and watched Red Skelton, The Honeymooners, and The Ed Sullivan Show before going to bed. Movies and television. Saturdays felt special.

Lincoln Elementary School on the near-west side exposed me to classroom learning for the first time. Kathy led me five blocks to and from school each day. The experience expanded my world, and the last portion of our walk included Shawano Avenue, one of Green Bay's busiest streets. I'd hit the big time. Overnight, I assumed the newfound maturity of a school kid. Negotiating Shawano Avenue's stoplights added a further sense of responsibility. I hadn't crossed busy streets alone before this and now it seemed routine. Pushing my worldly envelope to new limits brought excitement rather than fear, adventure rather than panic, and a sense of curiosity rather than trepidation.

During second grade, I changed from Lincoln Public School to Annunciation Catholic School. No sooner had I learned my way to and from the new classrooms than we moved again, across town and into another school district. SS Peter and Paul Catholic School introduced me to priests and nuns. A five-foot ball of venom by the name of Sister Aloysius routinely threw chalk-laden erasers at misbehaving fifth graders. A young priest who we called the "Duck" delivered predictably unintelligible homilies in a heavy Polish accent. The hair on the back of his head never laid flat and thus the nickname. Our parents, actually everyone, referred to him as the "Duck". The one time everyone seemed to understand him occurred on those Sundays when the Green Bay Packers played home games. He asked everyone to pray for the team, for the coaches to make good decisions, and for the players to perform better than their opponents. He mercifully kept the rest of his homily short on those special days.

The most memorable priest, Father Mauthe, connected with adults and kids alike. He'd been an orphan and that experience must have filled him with special powers. We all loved him.

Every school day began with a 7:30 a.m. mass. We knelt on solid wooden planks, learned to remain quiet, and enjoyed watching the Duck or listening to Fr. Mauthe.

Life for the next ten years turned out to be even more fun.

Normally, we rode a bus to and from school. I convinced Mom that it'd be easier for her if I rode a bicycle during the spring and fall months. The roads presented a dangerous obstacle as the shoulders seemed very narrow and the first half-mile consisted of a dangerous stretch with a higher speed zone. Nonetheless, I rode quite often. It freed me from adhering to a bus schedule, while at the same time, it opened a world of adventure in riding. Rainy days made little difference. Uncomfortable? Sure, but seldom to the point of convincing me to ride the bus.

One day, I decided to become an altar boy. Somehow, it took the pain out of sitting through morning mass. I moved around as an altar boy and stayed alert so I'd remember to ring the bells at the right time. Father Mauthe celebrated my first mass. He made it feel special and helped me through the rough spots. On Saturdays, I supported either funerals or weddings. I preferred funerals despite all the crying because when the mass ended everyone left rather quickly for the burial. Weddings, on the other hand, kept extending for pictures. No one seemed inclined to leave and that forced me to stay longer. At least everyone seemed happy and occasionally a good best man slipped a couple of bucks into our hands.

I tried piano lessons, but for me, playing seemed mechanical and awkward. My poor instructor tried in vain to infuse rhythm and tempo into my non-musical brain. I practiced little and it showed. Mediocrity felt uncomfortable.

Local Boy Scout Troop 18 held much greater interest. Several neighborhood playmates and I became scouts. Senior scouts told us we had to begin at the bottom of the totem pole, but would soon climb higher. We met other kids our age and embraced doing things as a group. Camping ranked as particularly fun. Everyone had specific duties, like gathering firewood or fetching water. We acquired woodland skills together and explored unknown forestlands.

Somewhere along the line, I realized that earning specific merit badges paved the way to further promotion. The requirements list seemed insurmountable. I'd have to chip away at it little by little, like a long hike taken one step at a time.

Each merit badge required a level of effort that at first glance appeared impossible. But with a bit of thought, research, and determination, completing the requirements became possible. An enormous lesson in life began to cement in my mind. Define the problem, put forth the required effort, and find success. If that doesn't work, then repeat the process. I became an Eagle Scout.

1968 National Boy Scout Jamboree at Valley Forge, PA

An incredibly memorable Boy Scouting event involved riding a bus to Valley Forge for the 1964 National Boy Scout Jamboree.

Two years before the Jamboree, Dad asked if I'd like to attend. My "yes" response prompted, "How are you going to pay for it?"

He then suggested that I start a landscaping business. He helped with the wording of flyers and two days later I kicked off my first entrepreneurial undertaking. Eight or ten neighborhood residents paid ten dollars for a day's work cutting and trimming their grassy slopes. These jobs seemed to be exclusively for the homes with large, near-vertical lawns. No wonder they wanted me to help. On most summer mornings, I pushed our lawnmower with gas can in hand, toward someone's ski-slope property.

Along the way, certain values formed and became part of my being. Values like serving the church as an altar boy and providing honest service by professionally cutting and trimming grass. I learned the value of setting goals, including becoming an Eagle Scout and paying my way to the 1964 National Jamboree. Vision coupled with determination made life interesting. Without either one, following the path of least resistance or worse, sitting idle, could have become far too easy.

Chapter 3

Skiing is the next best thing to having wings.
– Oprah Winfrey

WE DIDN'T WATCH TELEVISION. WE DIDN'T play games. We got out and did things. Spring arrived. Saturday's sunrise announced another adventure – trekking, exploring near and distant fields, farm visits, secret hide-out creations, or any other zany undertaking that piqued our interest. Hungry, growling stomachs brought us home for dinner, and later the first illuminated street light announced, "Time to head home."

The Brown County Mental Health Center, which we referred to as the Insane Asylum, housed a variety of older persons with mild mental health issues. In addition to a large hospital-like facility, the center operated a farm complete with cows, pigs, and expansive agricultural fields. Open access to the barns, and in particular the pigsty, quickly became our favorite stop. We always engaged one of the supervised patients before going inside just to be sure we wouldn't get in trouble. The sows grew to enormous size and we stood in awe gawking at them.

Are they dangerous? Do they bite?

We always seemed to spot one with a dozen piglets as cute as a litter of pups. The barns housed a variety of interesting animals.

Cows appeared much larger but didn't seem nearly as interesting to watch. The livestock barns blended aromas of straw, animals, and all the other smelly things scattered inside. Over time, the foreign and nasty smells became quite natural. After watching the barn animals, we'd hike out into the fields and beyond. Our destination always included streams several miles to the north. In the spring and fall, we'd try unsuccessfully to catch large salmon that swam there from the bay of Green Bay.

We never got tired while hiking endless miles, and fancied ourselves to be great explorers, like the early Frenchmen who'd been there many years before us.

Summer days passed without reference to clocks. The sun drifted across the sky or the moon illuminated the night. They provided all the time-keeping we needed. One year we caught gophers and named them Zorro or Grunt or some other catchy title. We kept them in homemade cages for a couple of days before letting them go free. The little buggers inflicted painful bites and each of us wore Band-Aids where one of them had chomped on a finger. Over time, each of us also visited the doctor's office for painful tetanus shots.

Pouring water down their hobbit-like holes initiated the capture process. Soon one scampered out toward another hiding place. The chase began. Gophers proved excellent zig-zag escape artists as we dived toward them with arms extended. A bite or two later and we'd have one under control.

Another year, we discovered a grassy field filled with slithering garden snakes. Over time, we became quite proficient at stepping on them before taking hold behind their heads and dropping them into an old rice bag. We emptied the field of what must have been fifty or more snakes before the summer ended.

Our limited supply of glass cages created a temporary snake-housing dilemma. Fortunately, our homes had basements with window wells that allowed light to illuminate the basement's interior. Their galvanized structure and three-foot depth also solved our snake-cage problem. That all changed one day when Mom moved the laundry from washer to dryer directly under our window well and noticed twenty snakes looking down at her.

The next day we released all the snakes into a wooded area well behind our house and never saw them again.

Winter snow and frigid air added a new dimension to our adventures. Daytime hikes continued over snow-drifted fields. We pulled a toboggan or wore cross-country skis and occasionally we brought along a thermos filled with hot cocoa. Eventually, our boots became wet or frozen and our feet needed relief. That discomfort eventually drew us back home.

Green Bay's recreation department operated a ski slope called Triangle Hill several miles from our house … close enough to reach on skis. Free admission made everything more accessible. The city maintained two rope tows and better yet, kept the slopes open until 10 p.m. most nights.

One night, my brother and I decided to ski to and from Triangle Hill. I plotted a shortcut through some hilly fields and across a single farm to the slopes. The hilly section, unfortunately, had drifted snow almost eight feet deep. We pushed our way through it very slowly and found ourselves near exhaustion upon reaching the ski hill. We recovered quickly, however, and skied until closing time.

The trip home felt slightly better as we'd already carved a path. Still, pushing along waist-deep in snow for an hour zapped our remaining energy. Eventually, we moved onto a road for the last portion of the trek. We never again took that shortcut. The fact that the shortcut existed in absolute darkness never fazed us.

Much of each winter included skiing at Triangle Hill. The city offered free ski lessons at the beginning of each ski season and my brother, sister, and I always volunteered to instruct beginner and intermediate students.

The closest commercial ski slopes existed three to four hours north. Our destination of choice became Iron Mountain in northern Michigan. On New Year's Day, I drove a carload of friends in our AMC Rambler American north to Iron Mountain. Knowing the temperatures would remain below zero the entire day didn't dissuade us.

Along the way, our radiator thermostat stuck, caused the radiator to overheat, and ultimately blew off the radiator cap. I pulled to the side of the road and waited until the radiator cooled before wedging an old t-shirt into where the cap had been. We continued. Every fifteen to twenty minutes we'd have to stop, let the radiator cool, and fill it with fresh water or snow before continuing. I never thought to have it fixed before returning home from the slopes.

We all suffered frostbitten cheeks. Two trips down the slopes became the maximum before heading into the chalet to thaw. Despite the cold, it began to snow. The trip home brought with it far greater danger than any of us could have imagined. The radiator issue required periodic stops during the entire trip but fortunately functioned well enough to eventually make it home. We drove in what turned out to be a developing blizzard. Everyone slumped in their seats, exhausted. The return drive lasted almost six hours.

These became carefree days when we threw caution to the wind. Heck, we didn't know what caution meant until we came face-to-face with the consequences of our "carefree" decisions. Common sense slowly took hold. The limits of where I sensed caution may have been a bit close to the danger zone, a consequence of having found myself there so often while learning life's limits.

Green Bay's Chicago and North Western train station.

A special week highlighted each summer. My sister, brother, and I bought coach tickets on Chicago and North Western's train from Green Bay to Milwaukee. We'd spend the next week doing "big city" things with our Aunt Ginnie, Uncle Gordy, and our cousins before returning home. The process of buying tickets involved dealing with a businesslike stationmaster and it always felt a bit intimidating. Boarding the train introduced us to a new world, one different from anything we'd experienced before. I never felt sad to be leaving home. Rather, my heart filled with anticipation of what lay ahead. The train's slow, smooth acceleration led us through back alleys and otherwise unseen sections of town. I imagined seedy characters who ventured into this mysterious realm. Through perilous twists and turns, we clickety-clacked into the farmlands. My mind jumped to new dreams. I loved those times and they included unique adventures.

I watched the Milwaukee Braves' Hank Aaron, Eddie Mathews, Joe Adcock, Warren Spahn, and Lew Burdette playing afternoon games in Milwaukee County Stadium. They appeared bigger than life. Seeing them in person filled the day with excitement. Later that same week, we'd gawk at the County Zoo elephants and stare into the monkey enclosure for what seemed like hours.

Chapter 4

The man on top of the mountain didn't fall there.
– Vince Lombardi

ONE SPRING, MOM AND DAD ENCOURAGED me to participate in city-wide Little League baseball. The league consisted of geographically split divisions throughout the city, but unfortunately, none of the teams existed close to home. I wouldn't know any of the other players and would have to bike five miles each way for practice and sometimes farther to play games. But if I performed well enough to make a team, I'd get a uniform, meet new kids, and have lots of fun. I attended all of the tryout sessions and felt like a pro when St. Phillips drafted me.

A two-hour practice commenced at 5 p.m. each Monday, Wednesday, and Friday. Unless it rained, I rode my bike five miles to the practice field. All the other players lived in the St. Phillips neighborhood, attended school together, and consequently knew each other. I instantly became an anomaly, an outsider who'd joined their team. We practiced together, ran laps around the outfield together, and embraced the same goals. It felt uncomfortable at first but I soon became one of them. Practice broadened my friendships and expanded my world geography. We practiced and played baseball. It couldn't get much better than this.

I discovered my baseball hand-eye coordination to be above average. On one Wednesday night, our moderately successful team faced the league's number-one pitcher,

John Diamond. John threw a sizzling fastball along with a moderately breaking curveball. He pitched a three-hitter that night and flummoxed all but one of our batters. I hit a double, a triple, and a home run, three bright spots in an otherwise disastrous outing. He threw the ball fast and accurately. It made hitting it easy if I started my swing a bit earlier than normal.

I played in the All-Star game each year. Neighborhood friends didn't know I played baseball, and I always felt they missed some of the best times summer had to offer. Of course, none of that mattered. I loved every minute of playing ball.

I also learned that finding the best things in life took effort. Seldom did opportunity simply fall into one's lap. I realized that putting forth the effort paid dividends beyond what I expected. Focused effort brought reward.

That's exactly what happened late in 1967.

1967 Green Bay Packers vs. Dallas Cowboys "Ice Bowl".

Mr. Ward happened to be the lead Sports Writer for the Green Bay Press-Gazette, and more importantly, found himself on my landscape customer list. The best part about cutting his lawn involved gawking at his son's sleek

Triumph T100C motorcycle. The worst part involved mosquitoes. Hordes of them viewed me as a blood bank ready for withdrawals. I know Mr. Ward appreciated having me deal with the pesky twits rather than doing it himself.

One day he called and asked if I'd be interested in volunteering to work the Packers National Football League Championship game on New Year's Eve.

"Yes! Of course, I'm interested. Wow, thanks."

He added that I could ask three of my friends to work as well. Mr. Ward began looking more and more like St. Peter welcoming me into heaven.

Game day. I hung press credentials around my neck and felt like the most important kid on the planet. The reason this game became so famous slapped me in the face as I stepped outside – Arctic cold. The game-time temperature hovered at minus fifteen degrees Fahrenheit with an average wind chill of minus forty-eight degrees. Stadium seating sold out. Twenty-five thousand fans huddled tight, drank beer, and cheered wildly to avoid frostbite.

My three friends didn't need press credentials as they remained outside helping cameramen handle rolls of film. Two of them worked along the top row of seats and the third endured even worse conditions atop the press box. At times during the game, various parts of their cameras froze. I worked inside the heated press box amid the Packer's play-by-play writers. Dallas reporters filled the seats in front of me, next to the front windows.

I delivered typed play-by-play sheets at the end of each quarter to the Associated Press telex office at the far end of the stadium. I found the job more entertaining than difficult, and at half-time, a policeman cleared me onto the playing field to make my delivery. The grass crunched underfoot in its frozen state.

During the game, ice accumulated on the press box windows, and the Dallas writers took turns scraping it away. What seemed like a normal cold day to me struck them as unworldly. I laughed inside as they complained.

"Here are the Packers, third down, inches to go, to paydirt. 17–14, Cowboys out in front, Packers trying for the go-ahead score. Starr begins the count. Takes the snap ... He's got the quarterback sneak and he's in for the touchdown and the Packers are out in front! 20–17! And 13 seconds showing on the clock and the Green Bay Packers are going to be ... World Champions, NFL Champions, for the third straight year!"
– Ted Moore, Packers' radio announcer.

Everyone, except the Dallas writers, cheered and danced around the press box. I hoped to sneak into the locker rooms and asked those in the press box if I could have their press credentials as souvenirs. Once I had three credentials in hand, I joined my frozen friends at the fifty-yard line and convinced them to follow me into the locker rooms.

The Cowboys' locker room doors remained open. I saw quarterback Don Meredith, receiver Lance Rentzel, and huge tackle Bob Lilly. We'd walked in somewhat confident like we belonged. We could've heard a pin drop, not because we didn't belong but because disappointment permeated the air. No one talked, and few moved about. Maybe the Packer's room would feel more exciting ...

A security guard stopped us despite our official press credentials. A cameraman passed. I told the guard we handled film for that guy. He looked at us big-eyed kids with the experience of a lifetime within reach and nodded ever so slightly. We didn't waste time. It felt crowded. Reporters huddled around Bart Starr asking questions as he removed his shoulder pads. Ray Nitschke sat alone on a training table unwrapping adhesive tape from his wrists. He smiled and I noticed gaps where quite a few of his teeth should have been. The dark grease under his eyes exaggerated an already tough appearance.

Nitschke suffered frostbitten feet. His toenails eventually fell off and his toes turned purple. Bart Starr had frostbite on his fingers as did many others. Yeah, it felt cold alright. Everyone called it the "Ice Bowl."

What a game! What a day!

Chapter 5

A child needs freedom within limits.
– Maria Montessori

NEIGHBORHOOD PARENTS FELT THAT OUR Lady of Premontre High School offered a healthy balance of academics, religious education, and after-school activities. Norbertine priests rode herd on the eight hundred or so all-male students. They brought an unwavering level of discipline to their classrooms, a fact that parents seemed to especially appreciate. The fact that it existed across the Fox River on the far-west side of town hadn't impacted Mom and Dad's decision. Between ride-sharing and city buses, transportation never felt like a major issue. During the warmer time of the year, I convinced my parents to let me ride my bike to school. Although I did this on occasion, the ten-mile ride took so long that I had to start toward school at a ridiculously early hour and I returned home well after dark. Although my Schwinn three-speed enjoyed high ratings, it plodded along in the subsonic realm much slower than today's feather-weight ten-speeds.

The morning bus, which picked us up two miles from home, followed a circuitous route for an hour before letting us off in front of the school. The evening buses required a single transfer in the middle of Green Bay and dropped us off two miles short of home. Walking the last segment at times felt refreshing, other times it stole away project and homework time and usually bordered on torture during cold or windy rain storms. Winter walks never felt as bad because we always dressed appropriately. Passing drivers, heartless morons at times, occasionally splashed icy-cold slush against our legs. We'd hitch-hike more often than not.

While some interesting activities simply couldn't fit into an already busy schedule, we made room for others. Each year I auditioned for the school play. These events became major productions and attracted a broad audience. The music director once told me to sing softly, confirming that my unbridled and undisciplined attempts at harmony had not gone unnoticed. One year, I performed as an acrobat in The Music Man. Twisting through the air suited my talents much better than singing.

Intramural basketball reinforced my love of team sports. Our eight-man squad of short-shooters became close both on-court and off. We'd play most games on Saturday mornings and that freed me from home chores until much later in the day. That alone justified all the effort of getting to and from school on the weekends.

I practiced with the varsity football team for a week. On the fourth day, I participated in a drill where two burley linemen led an equally large running back toward me and another tackler. Nope. Crazy contact sports lost my interest. Next on the list … Track.

It didn't take long to realize that my running style leaned toward quick and shifty rather than smooth and fast. High-jumping and pole-vaulting offered a more suitable challenge. I became a competitive high-jumper on those occasions when the competition dipped to my level. Only when my legs stretched and gained springiness could I clear a bar higher than five feet. Maybe if I reincarnated I'd improve. Anything over five feet represented a bridge too far. Pole-vaulting, on the other hand, became the event that occupied my dreams.

The entire track and field program centered on basic old-school ideals, starting with our coach.

Ted Fritsch played running back for the Green Bay Packers from 1942 to 1950. Why he became a track coach rather than a football coach, I'll never know, but I'm thankful for his choice. His huge frame at first appeared a bit soft, but in fact, it retained an impressive underlying muscle tone. We loved his fatherly character, his tobacco chews, and his obvious love of life. When he ran down the pole vault path with a large bamboo pole to demonstrate basic techniques, we watched in awe. To see him clear any height amazed us. We locked onto every word he said and convinced ourselves that we too could do what he demonstrated.

Bamboo and aluminum poles imposed a simplified technique … speed and a swinging motion transformed into height. During my senior year, the school bought two fiberglass poles and techniques suddenly changed.

I started practicing as soon as possible after classes and quite often found myself alone on the track after everyone else departed. My parents insisted I stop training at 6 p.m. so that I could get home by 8 p.m. During my senior year, I placed third in the state track meet.

When I turned sixteen, Dad suggested I think about getting a job and earning some extra money. I applied at the nearest Red Owl Grocery Store and several days later received a call and a job offer. I earned $1.10 per hour stuffing groceries into paper bags, stocking shelves, and stamping prices on products. I eventually joined the overnight floor scrubbing team, which for some odd reason felt like a promotion.

Green Bay Red Owl grocery store where I learned customer service and hard work.

A new dimension of discipline and honesty took shape without my ever hearing words of guidance. I'd show up for work on time or notify the manager of the delay. My lateness affected others because someone involuntarily covered my shift past their normal quitting time. This imposition finally hit home when I worked additional hours because someone else called in sick. Idle time became wasted time. The company paid me to work and for the most part, that's what I did.

I filled open time with lifeguard duties at the community swimming pool. Pool membership included families living in the neighborhood, and keeping all those kids happy hinged on finding lifeguards. They seemed hard to hire for some reason, probably because the daily pay barely covered the cost of a decent meal. As long as no one floundered in the water or became too rowdy, lifeguard duty felt easy, even though the responsibility remained high.

Days sitting in a raised chair above the swimming pool became fewer and fewer after Ted Fritsch hired me as a roustabout at Green Bay's Bay Beach Amusement Park.

The park attracted families with its scenic views at the mouth of the Fox River. It featured bumper cars, two small-scale passenger train rides, a large slide, and a Ferris wheel. A single concession sold a ready supply of ten-cent popcorn bags and five-cent sticks of cotton candy. Its large pavilion sold prepared food and hosted community dances, movies, and other events.

Bay Beach Amusement Park Miniaturized Train Station.

Work stretched from pre-dawn past dusk. Tasks universally included greasy, sweat-caked pulling, pushing, or lifting. In my mind, Bay Beach represented heaven on earth.

Weekend duty began at 4 a.m. when we'd open the concession stand and start popping corn. Batch after batch filled small brown bags and we stacked those into larger cylindrical barrels. By mid-morning families appeared. Happy. Full of energy. Rides opened, and the entire park came to life with picnics and child-centered entertainment.

Some days the pavilion required reconfiguration – clearing and stacking a hundred long tables with chairs to clear the floor for dancing. Two days later the reverse occurred.

Every day ended in exhaustion. I've mentally thanked Coach Fritsch over and over again for this opportunity. It reinforced the lessons of hard work. With great effort comes great reward. Without it, life remains dull.

High school summers consisted of packing grocery bags and performing lifeguard duties during the week, scrubbing floors on Friday nights until 1 a.m., and working as a roustabout at Bay Beach all day Saturday and Sunday.

My younger brother and I loved fishing. The season started in the spring with rainbow smelt runs, then summer fishing for perch and walleyes, and concluded in the fall with salmon runs. Ice fishing provided an additional option during the winter months although we tended to focus more on the ski slopes.

Smelt migrated from Lake Michigan into tributaries before spawning. As winter temperatures climbed above the thirties, the run began. The exact timing of the annual smelt run became a popular topic. We'd wait with dip nets, buckets, and waders until the rumors turned favorable. Dipping for smelt occurred at night in cold air. Shorelines bristled with excitement as fishermen harvested buckets of the little devils.

Each summer, along with my dad and brother, I'd head north into Canada with a canoe strapped atop our car. Boundary Waters is a million-acre wilderness area within the Superior National Forest in northern Minnesota. Quetico Provincial Park abuts it on the Canadian side of the border and stretches sixty miles from east to west and forty miles from north to south. Hundreds of lakes and rivers link together via 550 more-or-less maintained portages. Its rugged beauty includes beaver homes, wandering moose, and a rare assortment of eagles, hawks, and cranes. Only once or twice in all our excursions did we encounter other people.

Atikokan Headquarters marked our entry point into this remote world of natural beauty. We'd dip our loaded canoes into icy-clear waters and begin ten days of paddling into the unknown … and catch fresh fish for each dinner.

Pre-GPS navigation consisted of map reading and prayer. Bears viewed fishermen as a source of food so we camped on tiny islands. Even then, a curious bear might swim our way in search of raspberries or improperly stored food.

Father and son stories blended with a crackling fire and entertained us most nights. Chores naturally divided among us. Dad cooked, I cleaned up afterward, and my brother did whatever odd jobs arose.

Surviving in the wilderness seemed natural to us. We knew the basics of creating a shelter, staying warm, finding food, and starting a fire. We knew that doing it in winter would not be easy.

Mom and Dad planned several special family vacations. Our first major trip occurred during the summer of 1963 and included a flight from Chicago to Ontario. From there, we rented a car and drove to Nova Scotia. It marked the first time I'd been in an airplane, and it felt like magic, like being with Aladdin on his flying carpet. As the ground disappeared below and behind us, a new world of clouds and crisp blue skies opened before my eyes.

Chapter 6

Eighty percent of the final exam will be based on the one lecture you missed and the one book you didn't read.
– Unknown

NOW WHAT ... COLLEGE OR THE MILITARY draft? Like most high school seniors, I thought of taking an academic break and applying for some fun jobs. That mental image shifted from bright and sunny to a dismayed chill when the inevitability of being drafted clarified my reality. Army or Marines? Vietnam jungles. Venomous creatures, punji stakes, bullets, and bombs ... or classes, studying, the status quo.

The first two years of my liberal arts program flew by rather quickly at the University of Wisconsin's extension campus in Green Bay. During the second year, soccer replaced intramural basketball as the school sport. Several international students received scholarships because they possessed world-class ball-handling skills. I met them while scrimmaging in a nearby park and soon found myself in awe of their abilities. Learning better techniques elevated my game from a brute force, bump-and-grind approach to one that included more thought and finesse. They introduced me to a sport I loved to play for years into the future.

Another odd college twist came with the watercolor painting that I first pursued in high school. I found mental balance and personal satisfaction in creating landscapes of our northern lakes and fields. Eventually, I amassed a collection of paintings and brought them to gatherings where I hustled a few bucks for unframed creations. The sales paid for my school books.

Over time, I established a favorable artistic reputation and found myself accepting commissions to paint large wall-sized acrylic murals. I discovered that painting combined with meditation infused feelings into the landscapes that I visualized. As with so many things, time became the enemy of creativity. Enough of it simply didn't exist.

I moved to Madison, Wisconsin, and attended the main campus of the University of Wisconsin. For the first time in my life, I found myself alone and singularly responsible for my academic success. Envision two locomotives racing toward each other on a single track, or some early six-winged aircraft trying to get airborne. Superimpose my picture on the result.

The first time I sat alone in my tiny dorm room, I experienced the hollow feeling of isolation. Nothing felt familiar. My parents remained only hours away in Green Bay but may as well have been living on the moon. The campus suddenly felt foreign, and I had no close friends. The feeling passed when my roommate arrived, a geeky math major named Douglas. Within the week I began working at the cafeteria, scrubbing the largest pots and pans I'd ever seen. When one pot had been scraped and scrubbed clean of its baked-on grime, another one showed up. It continued for hours and constituted hard work.

Douglas and I seldom saw each other as our schedules varied so much. I'd go out at night and he'd study. Then he disappeared after suffering a bleeding ulcer and being admitted to the hospital. He remained there for most of the semester.

Classrooms scattered themselves across a sprawling campus. Walking from one to the next felt refreshing during summer months when warm breezes cooled the air.

However, bitter cold January winds required fortitude, and carrying a handful of books with frozen fingertips took a higher level of commitment. Several classes consisted of more than three hundred students and caused me to question the value of such mass-produced learning.

I concocted what at the time seemed to be a perfect alternative. I'd get assignments on day one, conduct research in the library, study in my room, and walk to class only for quizzes and final exams. To my dismay, the plan resulted in academic probation. Ironically, the determining grade for probation had been an "F" in Watercolor 201. The professor demanded one-hundred-percent attendance which I found more unproductive than educational. He warned me and I didn't heed his words. Something Will Rogers once said came to mind.

"Things will get better – despite my best efforts to improve them."

A four-year University of Wisconsin campus opened in Green Bay later that same year and seemed like a good place to study my way back from academic probation. Rather than feel depressed or defeated, I felt challenged climbing out of the hole I'd dug, taking control of what I could control, and not worrying too much about the rest. I called home and explained the situation and that I planned to return for at least the next year. My renewed zeal for classroom participation and evening study sessions paid dividends. I graduated with a degree in Community Science and managed to resurrect a respectable grade point average.

That first venture from home taught me failure. It taught me not to quit, but to adjust, re-engage, and persist.

Attending mass every Sunday and often during the week had always been a part of my life. As I grew older, I wondered about the relevance of the sermons I heard. They generally focused on biblical recollections and the priest's interpretation of things. More often than not, I'd get lost.

Things changed, thank goodness. Our family attended mass at the Ecumenical Center, a non-denominational facility organized by my old mentor Fr. Mauthe. He intended to provide religious services that seemed more in tune with the needs of local college students. He soon gained an enthusiastic following. In large part, his success stemmed from "in-touch" homilies. He extracted the essence of the scripture and applied it to contemporary issues within the region or nation. He adeptly led a mixed audience to think about current issues from a moral and religious perspective.

Life-long friendships formed at the Ecumenical Center. Religion never stifled anything. Rather, it gave a better perspective, one rooted in positive thought rather than anger, mistrust, hate, or a "damned if you don't" perspective. Instead of avoiding Sunday mass, I found myself welcoming it.

As I prepared to graduate from college, a life-altering decision stared me in the face. Would I request a religious deferment and enter a seminary, would I flee to Canada and live there for the rest of my life, or would I enlist in the military with a promise of Officer's Training School?

Simply waiting to be drafted seemed a foolish course of non-action. I knew deep inside that serving my country represented the right choice for me, even though I had little idea of what the future held. There seemed to be significantly more danger than security along the path before me. I'd been told that helicopter pilots in Vietnam, on average, survived six flights before being shot down. Yikes! How could the number be that low? Who in their right mind would volunteer to fly helicopters during a war? My parents surely worried about my choice of career fields and thus I never shared this unsubstantiated statistic. The Vietnam War raged on and none of us wanted to risk life or limb in that conflict.

I'd acquired the basic knowledge and psychological strength to become a pilot. My application for the United States Air Force Officer's Training School came back approved with an initial choice of becoming a helicopter pilot or a navigator. I could train as a pilot and fly helos for four years after which I'd cross-train into jets, or I could become a navigator.

Navigator seemed to be the safe choice. We'd all heard stories of helicopter pilots being shot down somewhat routinely in Vietnam. Nonetheless, I wanted to be a pilot so the choice became a "no-brainer." Of course, I'd be a helicopter pilot.

Chapter 7

Art by Lt Col Ed Cooke from the MAC Flyer, 1985

"The thing is, helicopters are different from planes. An airplane by its nature wants to fly, and if not interfered with too strongly by unusual events or by a deliberately incompetent pilot, it will fly. A helicopter does not want to fly. It is maintained in the air by a variety of forces and controls working in opposition to each other, and if there is any disturbance in this delicate balance the helicopter stops flying, immediately and disastrously.

"There is no such thing as a gliding helicopter.

"This is why being a helicopter pilot is so different from being an airplane pilot, and why, in general, airplane pilots are open, clear-eyed, buoyant extroverts, and helicopter pilots are brooders,

introspective anticipators of trouble. They know if something bad has not happened, it is about to."
– Harry Reasoner

LATE 1971. ANOTHER TENDERFOOT COLLEGE grad survived the shock of Officer Training School. I became a green-behind-the-ears United States Air Force 2nd Lieutenant and awaited the start of helicopter pilot training. Before long, I packed everything and hit the road. My destination, Mineral Wells, Texas.

On an early Saturday morning, my four-wheeled Volkswagen-with-a-Porsche 911-label rolled out of Lackland Air Force Base for the last time. A frisky little monkey I'd named Charley occupied the seat next to me. He'd been a spur-of-the-moment purchase and became my quirky companion.

I immediately sensed his trepidation. Hell, I felt nervous too, imagining the unknowns I'd likely gotten myself into by choosing to fly helicopters. Two of us, unsure of our future and without a care in the world, headed north.

Buying a car became a necessity and paying for it seemed easy enough. I raked in a bi-weekly windfall of $530.70 – before taxes. Hazardous duty pay, subsistence, and quarters allowances added another $267.98. After a few quick calculations, I realized I could afford a car if I ate peanut butter and jelly sandwiches and drank a bit less beer. I could live with such a plan.

"Oh my god," I mumbled to myself the first time I drove down Mineral Wells' Main Street. It could have won the World Travel Award for the *Most Authentic Tumbleweed Community*. A half-mile facade of old-western storefronts defined its character. If Doc Holiday had stumbled out from one of them it would've appeared normal. I found Wolters

Army Air Field several blocks from town, and stumbled across Bodiford Trailer Park, my destination, conveniently nearby. While gawking out the window at some dilapidated bar and its oversized cowboy boot signage, I noticed the Bodiford Used Car lot, and behind it, the partially hidden trailer park. Unit #6 became home-sweet-home for the next six months.

2nd Lt Rick McCourt, a New York native and a friend from "casual status" at Officer's Training School had been assigned to the class immediately preceding mine. He arrived several weeks earlier and rented this rickety, cheap-looking box with beds. As I pulled to a stop, Rick bolted through the trailer door with a beer in hand.

"This area is relatively crime-free," he announced, "and more importantly, it's convenient. Come on in and grab a beer."

Who knew anything about Mineral Wells? Not me. I learned that in 1919, the town hosted the Chicago White Sox spring training camp. That year the "Black Sox" gambling scandal involved Shoeless Joe Jackson. It didn't look like much of a baseball town to me, and I never did see a baseball park. Over time, Mineral Wells became more famous for its paranormal incidents. You could join a Saturday afternoon haunted-house tour of the Crazy Water Hotel and the Haunted Hill House and then walk the halls of the Baker Hotel after dark. According to rumor, all of these places retained ghosts as current boarders. The downtown area felt comfortable and reflected the best of small-town America.

The 1970 U.S. Census pegged Mineral Wells' headcount at 18,411 which only slightly outnumbered the municipal rattlesnake population. It began a sharp decline shortly after Rick and I departed and continued declining for several years thereafter. Most of the Fort Wolters military and contractor personnel left town when the installation closed two months after our training ended. We never looked back.

It's said that first impressions are lasting. The U.S. Army Primary Helicopter School implanted a mental image of rural Texas that remains vivid in my mind to this day. It started at the U.S. Highway 180 gate leading into Fort Wolters. This grand entrance featured two orange-colored helicopters mounted on facing pedestals. To the left, an old Hiller OH-23 "Raven" had seen better days. Across from it, a TH-55A "Osage" appeared comparatively tiny, more like a toy than an aircraft. We called it the Mattel Messerschmidt and it'd be the aircraft soon scaring the bejesus out of us while at the same time solidifying our love of flight. The whole place struck me as both austere and sizzling.

In addition to a handful of Air Force and Army aviation cadets, Warrant Officer Candidates underwent rigorous leadership studies along with helicopter academic and flight training. I felt sorry for those guys. They barely had time to absorb the joy of their first flights as they lived far more restrictive lives than ours. Thankfully, their spit-and-shine drill instructors left us alone in our slightly less stressful world.

Fort Wolters also boasted an interesting history in that Audie Murphy completed his basic training there. During World War Two, Ft Wolters served as a German POW camp, and not surprisingly, our facilities appeared to be the originals. Our classrooms could easily have been old wooden barracks.

Class 72-34 wore brown hats and consisted of eleven Air Force and twenty-five Army Lieutenants. The Army guys seemed just like us despite not wearing the same type of flight suits. We'd become recent college grads and assembled at this place primarily because our alternative had been to become jungle-fighting infantrymen.

We struggled with academics, which included maintenance, aerodynamics, flying safety, navigation, weather interpretation, and radio procedures. Helicopters abused the most basic aerodynamic principles to the point that even the father of modern-day physics, Sir Isaac Newton, would've scratched his head. For example, as the rotor blades spun through the air, they constantly changed pitch. When the rotor blade traveled forward, the relative airflow across it increased because of the forward motion of the helicopter. As it swung to the rear, its pitch increased to compensate for its slower movement through the relative air mass. Without this correction, the helicopter would roll over in flight. The large rotating blades exacerbated gyroscopic properties such as precession. Inputs had to be applied ninety degrees before they'd take effect. Our instructor called it the Euler Angle Rule. Nobody fully understood it.

After sitting through a month of long academic days, we boarded a World War Two vintage school bus and headed to the main heliport where three hundred piston-powered Mattel Messerschmidts awaited us. Additional heliports named Downing and Dempsey Field hosted even more helos. Dempsey accommodated twenty-six rows of sixteen helicopters parked side-by-side. From these main heliports, we'd fly to stage fields with names like Pinto, Mustang, and

Wrangler. In previous years when Vietnamese pilots trained here, stage fields included names like Ben Hoa, Cam Ranh, and Da Nang. Most had been deactivated in parallel with a decreasing level of foreign training. From the stage fields, we qualified for practice at remote landing zones marked with different colored tires. White-tire zones identified easy landings, yellow zones became more difficult, and red tires highlighted the greatest landing challenge.

Heliports supported more than three hundred helicopters. I flew several of them.

Chapter 8

The only mystery in life is why the kamikaze pilots wore helmets.
– Al McGuire

OUR FIRST DAY OF FLIGHT FILLED EVERYONE with excitement. Nerves gripped my stomach. I worried I'd forget the checklist and become ham-fisted on the controls. Hopefully, this little toy-like machine would let me keep control. The engine rpm increased to take-off power. We lifted straight up to a three-foot hover. It felt like magic.

Half the instructors appeared to be young, type-A U.S. Army aviators. The other half consisted of relatively mellow Southern Airways of Texas contractors. I found myself assigned to one of the latter, a seventy-year-old glider enthusiast by the name of Mr. Chance. Somewhere along the way he'd become a helicopter instructor pilot and inherited me as one of his more challenging students. I noticed that the younger instructors respected him. It convinced me from the start to listen carefully to everything he said. On our first flight, he simulated an engine failure by suddenly retarding the throttle, unannounced. He'd briefed me that if this happened, I should immediately lower the collective and step on the right rotor pedal. That's exactly what I did! Except, I stomped the wrong pedal. We corkscrewed downward as the nose snapped toward the earth below and everything abruptly twisted 120 degrees to the left. It felt like we'd tumbled …

Mr. Chance grabbed the controls and calmly recovered, but I know his heart must have been pounding.

"We'll have to work on that," he said, and we continued back to the heliport without further conversation. Well, he'd either teach me to stay right side up or he'd wash me out. Nonetheless, I liked him.

Every day brought a new adventure. I passed all the written tests and lie awake at night thinking about how to approach red-tire landing zones. One day, we flew to a remote ridgeline, landed, ventured onto a rocky ledge, and watched a red-tailed hawk circle above. Mr. Chance explained how wind and heat created updrafts and how the hawk took advantage of them. I swear, he could see the air. None of the other instructors explained things in such an effective, interesting way.

Hovering a TH-55 looked easy enough but that all changed.

"Okay, you've got the controls," Mr. Chance announced. The first moment felt reassuring.

"Yeah, I've got this …"

Then the orange monster slowly drifted right. Stick left. More right drift, and then suddenly to the left. Then back to the right.

"Oh no!"

"I've got it," he announced. Like magic, our Mattel Messerschmidt froze in space, motionless at three feet altitude.

Auto-rotations warranted their reputation of being fear-filled maneuvers. If the engine stopped working, we could still safely land by lowering the collective and falling out of the sky to a soft landing. That is if everything went according to plan.

Mr. Chance retarded the throttle to idle. The falling sensation gripped the pit of my stomach. We floated in our seats much like cresting the rise of a giant roller coaster for the first time. It became less dramatic and more exhilarating with repetition.

Each instructor taught two students. While one student flew the other would sit in a no-frills stage field facility and watch his classmate struggle. I'd have laughed watching others continually lose aircraft control, but I knew I'd likely perform just as poorly when my turn came. I stifled the urge.

Mr. Chance used a rather unique approach to hovering. While others flailed in their attempts to remain steady in a three-foot hover, I'd be flying rectangular traffic patterns to the runway. I never actually hovered but rather descended to one end of the runway and then continued forward at ten feet above ground to the far end where I'd climb higher for another circuit. Somewhere along the way I simply slowed to a stop and voila! I hovered. After almost killing Mr. Chance on our first flight, this seemed a much safer way to tame the mechanical monster.

Practice at the stage fields built a complex skill set in each of us. We learned precise control for landings and takeoffs. Instructors repeatedly threw in-flight emergencies at us. It became intense with little wasted time.

Without realizing exactly when it happened, I hovered and auto-rotated without over-controlling, and after six and a half hours of flying, I soloed. It rekindled the feeling of driving a car for the first time, only this felt much, much better. The sense of freedom, of moving about the skies like a bird, going only where I wanted to go, and landing when and where I wanted to land expanded a two-dimensional world into three.

Once we overcame the novelty of flying solo, a popular in-flight activity became landing somewhere out of sight, finding a couple of medium-sized rocks, and placing them on the co-pilot's seat. We then flew over the Brazos River and tossed the rocks out one at a time, bombing the water below. Smaller rocks worked best. During the actual bombing, we let go of either the collective or the cyclic to free a throwing hand.

1st Lt Tom Whitlow reached the pit of pilot infamy after he loaded a rock bomb so large that it'd take both hands to throw out. Of course, he couldn't do that in flight and ended up returning to the main heliport with it still occupying his co-pilot seat. Only then did he realize that he couldn't leave it in the seat, or hope it'd go unnoticed sitting on the relatively spotless tarmac. In either case, he'd be discovered and disciplined.

His on-the-spot solution included repeating the post-flight inspection over and over again until all other helicopters landed and their pilots left the area. An hour later he continued inspecting, eventually lugging the rock two hundred yards to the far edge of the concrete tarmac and unceremoniously depositing it in the dirt. The rest of us sat on the bus waiting … waiting. We thought he must have gotten lost or heaven forbid, crashed. The instructors somehow understood.

On weekends, Rick and I drove separately to Fort Worth in search of interesting attractions. The Fort Worth Botanical Gardens soon became one of my favorites. It offered long walks along wooded pathways that wove in and out of beautiful, vibrant gardens. I'd lie on my back in grassy areas and dream about flying around billowy clouds as they floated past.

We'd reunite at Billy Bob's bar complex in the Fort Worth Stockyard around 5 p.m. The place turned out to be incredible, especially when seen through the eyes of a small-town kid from Wisconsin. Beautiful cowgirls served enormous char-broiled steaks, live bands bellowed country-western music, mechanical bulls entertained others, and a full-blown rodeo never seemed to end. After a couple of beers, we felt like homespun Texans.

That routine changed the weekend 2nd Lt Terry Amstuz met an American Airlines stewardess trainee at the Nutcracker Bar in Fort Worth. His chance encounter led to ten blind dates – helicopter pilots and airline stewardesses. What could possibly go wrong with this equation?

Terry attained temporary "hero" status. Unfortunately, within several weeks, most of the couples parted ways, myself included. My roommate, Rick, persisted in being the notable exception and maintained an intense telephone relationship for several months. Heartbreak arrived when his sweetheart discovered the pay difference between a military helicopter pilot trainee and a fully certified airline transport pilot. Rick sulked, emotionally drained … for all of a week.

Flight training remained center-stage. After several months of landing at progressively more difficult red zones, learning basic navigation, and reacting to endless emergency simulations, I graduated from basic helicopter training. I'd soon move to Dothan, Alabama, and begin the advanced course which included flying by referencing only the onboard instruments. Rick had already departed and surprisingly, I only saw him a couple of times after that. Uncharacteristically, our paths separated. We pursued a similar career but led different lives.

Before packing the car and embarking on the two-day trek to Alabama, I gave Charley to a family with two young boys. Charley, without question, found a more stable life in Mineral Wells. I often asked myself what possessed me to purchase him in the first place.

Chapter 9

You haven't seen a tree until you've seen its shadow from the sky.
– Amelia Earhart

DOTHAN FILLED SEVERAL SQUARE MILES amid acres upon acres of dusty cotton fields. Conjure up an image of the Deep South, you'd envision Dothan. Oppressively hot, humid air baked us during the day and stuck to us at night. Fort Rucker existed closer to Enterprise and Dale, but the sergeant who gave us directions must have known that finding Dothan would be vastly easier.

I drove twenty-five miles out of town before signs announcing Fort Rucker's main gate appeared. An Army sergeant at the billeting office assigned me to a spartan but adequate room on the third floor. I unpacked my few clothes and took the weekend to venture around the post. Nothing other than the giant Boll Weevil Monument in downtown Enterprise captured my attention. There didn't seem to be local stores or restaurants or anything that resembled a bar. By Sunday night, I convinced myself that I'd found the geographic center of nowhere. In a twisted way, the austerity proved to be perfect. Four months of concentrated learning commenced.

The Vietnam War raged on the far side of the planet. We sensed ourselves being drawn toward the conflict. Fort Rucker percolated a seriousness toward flying. The sprawling Officer's Club added a unique "spare no expense" dimension.

While I'm not a big fan of bingo, the Rucker O' Club's Wednesday bingo night changed lives. When I first drove past the club, I noticed a seventy-thousand-dollar Cessna 172 Skyhawk on display. Win the Club's "cover all" bingo game and the aircraft becomes yours. On the first week, a bingo caller declared fifty numbers and incremented that by one number each week until somebody won. After some lucky guy won the airplane, a Corvette Stingray pulling a large speedboat showed up as the next grand prize. Wives loved it, and husbands drank enough beer to float the speedboat to the Gulf Coast. What a madhouse. I naively participated a couple of times and found the crowds to be overwhelming and annoying. I preferred the quiet pleasure of eating a barbeque beef plate at some quiet roadside diner. It's hard to believe but studying became a preferred alternative.

1940's Link Aviation "Blue Box" trainer.

WALK RUN FLY

The first phase of advanced training involved flying with total reference to aircraft instruments. Before thrashing about the skies with blinders securely fastened, we did it in a classic first-generation simulator. When our turn came, each of us climbed into a wooden Link "blue box" trainer. Basic instruments in the cockpit occasionally responded to an instructor's inputs and usually responded to the pilot's control inputs. We hated these sessions because they felt so primitive and caused vertigo. Their limited value had nothing to do with our training but rather with setting the stage for future systems that more accurately simulated instrument flight and introduced complex emergencies.

Hundreds of war-torn UH-1D Hueys populated Rucker's various tarmacs. Their patched bullet holes validated them as real helicopters. Olive-drab camouflage looked more appropriate than the orange-painted Mattel Messerschmidts or OH-13s that we flew in training.

The thought of flying these "real" beasts fueled my desire for phase II training. But first, I'd need to pass an instrument check-ride in one of the orange-painted OH-13s. These old helicopters featured a large, distinctive plastic bubble surrounding its cockpit. One of them appeared in the opening scene of the TV series M*A*S*H while it delivered Korean War patients.

Learning instrument procedures under the bubble in Alabama's summer heat quickly became incredibly uncomfortable. Doing it with a hooded contraption designed to eliminate all outside references made it worse. Several Army students dropped out of training. Instructors constantly reminded us that flying in Vietnam would be worse so we should get used to it.

For me, every flight ended with a thumping headache. In time, I passed my instrument check ride and said "Hello" to the olive-drab Huey.

The exhilaration of tactical flying instantly erased memories of those pesky headaches. Life became an adrenalin rush. I mastered unannounced auto-rotations into pre-approved fields known only to the instructors. I did ninety-degree, 180-degree, and 360-degree turning auto-rotations. I once pulled the nose up, descended backward, and dumped the nose to regain forward speed for the landing. More often than not, we landed in a pasture or a farmer's field. The most dramatic simulated engine failures occurred while skimming trees at fifty feet. Straightforward pilot actions slowed the aircraft above the trees for as long as possible before letting it settle into whatever lay beneath. Of course, we always decelerated to a previously unseen field. I found it exhilarating.

Phase Two completion marked the end of helicopter qualification training. I received my wings and promptly headed to Dothan where I took the FAA Commercial Pilot exam. Later that day, I possessed a Commercial Pilot – Rotorcraft – Instrument rating.

As an Air Force pilot, I entered a two-week training session to learn a tactical air navigation system called TACAN. The Army didn't use this system so those classmates left for specialized helicopter checkouts shortly after graduation. The Air Force students' final aircraft assignments and locations would be awarded after completion of TACAN training.

The assignment process ultimately set the future path for each of us. We competed for one of eleven assignments and made the choice based on our class ranking. The first two selections would be HH-53s known as Super Jolly Green Giant helicopters. The assignment location would be Thailand. The remaining helicopters consisted of a CH-3 Jolly Green Giant destined for South Korea, UH-1s supporting stateside missile sites, and a single HH-43 Huskie destined for northern Thailand. I selected the CH-3.

Before moving to Utah for CH-3E training, I first traveled to Fairchild AFB near Spokane, Washington, for survival, evasion, resistance, and escape training. The two-week course didn't allow time for sightseeing. On the other hand, I'd be trekking through the cold, snowy mountains of the Northwest.

I had no idea what to expect. The survival and evasion portion included an overnight map-reading trek through Washington State's mountain wilderness. I instantly found it beautiful and invigorating. It reminded me of our family fishing adventures in the Canadian outback. Resistance and evasion training came next. The fun hiking part gave way to a moderately painful couple of days. Fortunately, the experience only simulated wartime prison life.

CH-3E helicopter training felt far more relaxed. The routine required the same study and focus, except it happened in beautiful Ogden, Utah. We learned the nuances of mountain flying and practiced instrument procedures over and over again. Toward the end of most flights, we'd overfly local ski resorts and assess their crowds. When we flew early morning sorties, we'd occasionally have the afternoon off, and we'd ski whenever the opportunity arose.

In addition to weekday skiing, I got hooked on photographing mountain goats, elk, and moose. It required trekking deep into the mountains with a camera. Over time, I became proficient in slogging along while wearing snowshoes. Breaking a trail through six feet of fresh powdered snow, regardless of how I did it, zapped a lot of energy. Trekking alone in the mountains so far from major roads may have been dangerous, but it soothed my adventurous spirit. I always found my way home, satisfied but exhausted.

My girlfriend from Wisconsin visited Utah for a week, and we explored much of the area together. While we enjoyed the time, I realized how distracted and self-focused I'd become. All my thoughts centered on flying, learning about the Air Force, and developing a healthy independence. Finding a companion and making a personal commitment would have to wait until later in life.

Chapter 10

… most people think that flying a plane is dangerous, except pilots don't because they know how easy it is.
– Fifth-grade student at Jefferson School, Beaufort, S.C.

ASIA QUIETLY AWAITED. I'D BEEN IN Wisconsin visiting family and sensed a subtle change in my relationships. Old drinking buddies had never left Wisconsin. They didn't think about world issues. National-level issues didn't warrant much attention either. I'd changed. Without knowing it, this newfound global perception became more focused. Green Bay, Wisconsin, no longer felt like the center of my universe, but rather a favorite place in a much more expansive world.

Most of my friends had never seen a real helicopter. I now flew them. They'd met people from our four-state region, but I trained shoulder to shoulder with guys from across the U.S. None of this changed how I viewed my Green Bay friends nor did it give me any sense of superiority. It did hammer home the point that my life-view had changed, a lot.

I boarded a flight from Green Bay to Los Angeles and ventured into the unknown. A friend from San Antonio met me at the airport and together we explored California's coastal State Route 1 to San Francisco. From there we found our way to Travis Air Force Base. I checked into billeting and waited two days for a departure flight.

The Boeing 707 in which I spent the next twenty-four hours shoe-horned a passenger into each cramped seat. Never had I been on such a long flight. We eventually landed at Osan Air Base, exhausted. South Korea appeared more rural than Wisconsin with rice paddies replacing cornfields. Pungent smells stung my nose. Whiffs of human feces from recently fertilized fields mixed with the unique smell of fermented kimchi stored on the roofs of every house. I wanted to fly operational missions, to do something other than train.

For the next thirteen months, I delivered supplies to remote mountaintop radar sites and transported VIPs, and when not doing that, I practiced instrument procedures. Mountain-top landing pads often consisted of little more than a twenty-foot concrete slab poured along some jagged ridgeline. If morning fog didn't shroud the mountains on calm days, swirling winds played with our stability. Landings presented the greatest challenge. Warming mountain air shot upward into billowy clouds that obscured approach paths and percolated turbulence. We maneuvered right or left, fought the bumps, and somehow found our way safely to the ground.

One cold Saturday morning, we delivered six staff officers to a mountainous crest near Pohong along the country's east coast. Describing the ground condition as "sloppy" doesn't describe it adequately. Foot-deep, crystallized, and half-frozen muck existed everywhere. Each officer had no alternative but to jump into the freezing mud. Of the six officers, five wore fatigues with high-topped boots. The last one wore office blues and high-gloss dress shoes. I witnessed the ten percent who didn't get the memo on field conditions.

The 33rd Aerospace Rescue and Recovery unit operated a short distance down the flight line from us. Their helicopter aircrews lived two buildings away from our dorm, and I often spent evenings at their hooch bar sharing stories. A fun-loving Lieutenant Colonel and newly assigned Second Lieutenant stopped by and talked a bit before their evening flight. It'd be our last conversation. They flew into a mountain sixty minutes later.

That represented my first close exposure to death. Darkness took my friends in an instant. The result impressed me as being abrupt and permanent. I felt empty and didn't know how to rationalize what'd happened. Ever since then, I've bottled up those emotions and suppressed them. It affected how I related to dying people later in life.

Returning to the United States for thirty days of vacation after completing half of a remote assignment seemed the norm for most others. I viewed it as a long trip for such a relatively short visit. Besides, I didn't miss home that much yet. Attending two weeks of Jungle Survival Training in the Philippines sounded like a much better option. I dropped into Taipei on the way back to Korea and spent a couple of days sightseeing.

Survival training included a helicopter ride to some remote mountain location where we spent a couple of nights sleeping in hammocks and eating whatever the jungle had to offer. When not bivouacking in the jungle, I stayed with a helicopter pilot friend I knew from Utah. I'd never been in a jungle before this and the experience brought new levels of heat and humidity. The flight to Taiwan transformed a sweltering jungle routine into a relatively temperate urban exploration – a nice change.

Taiwan created more vivid memories than expected. I'd directed a taxi driver to a non-descript, smoke-filled place called Genghis Khan Mongolian Barbeque. A crusty old Master Sergeant who'd eaten there the previous year had recommended it. Meaty-flavored steam rose from large cone-shaped steel plates where Mongol-like cooks seared shards of meat and vegetables using lengthy chopsticks. A three-foot layer of smoke along the ceiling combined with rising cigarette smoke. Chinese music accented an atmosphere that reeked of exotic Asia. A large Taiwanese beer and a bowl filled with Mongolian barbeque slowly disappeared as I relaxed while observing the crowd. I imagined myself in an old Chinese mystery movie.

The odd thing is that Mongolian barbeque isn't Mongolian. A Taiwanese man named Wu Zhaonan came up with the name. Wu at first wanted to call it Beijing barbeque, but because of political sensitivities settled for Mongolian barbeque.

I visited the National Museum without knowing exactly what to expect. Little did I know that nearly 700,000 pieces of Mainland Chinese artifacts and artworks existed inside. The treasure trove dates back to 1931 when Generalissimo Chiang Kai-shek ordered the National Palace Museum in the Forbidden City to prepare for evacuation. Half of the 13,941 crates along with 6,066 crates from his Summer Palace and the Imperial Hanlin Academy moved to Shanghai. Eventually, 2,972 Forbidden City crates rode on ships to Taiwan. These contained some of the most valuable pieces of the collection.

I stared in awe at what appeared to be a thin white thread. But when I viewed it under a microscope, I gawked at a linked chain that'd been carved from a fishbone. I stood in disbelief looking at ornately carved balls within balls, some fifteen layers deep. From tapestries to porcelain vases, the displays fascinated me.

One of the Chinese attendants told me they changed artifacts with items from their vast warehouse every few months. With so many pieces, it'd take almost twenty years before the current items appeared again.

Back in Korea, I realized how enriching my mid-tour vacation had been and how routine the flying had become

One day while returning from a radar site support mission, that abruptly changed.

"Sir, we've got a massive transmission oil leak!" my flight mechanic suddenly announced.

Without lubricating oil, the rotor blades would soon stop spinning, and that'd be a really bad thing.

"Crew, we're auto-rotating to one of those rice paddies below us. Hang on!"

… and down we went. We landed safely and radioed home so a rescue mission could be organized.

Korean policemen approached and finding us uninjured, proceeded to cordon off curious farmers. I felt like the lead character on a Korean War movie set. Eventually, a helicopter maintenance team landed next to us, changed the oil line that had failed, and led us back to Osan Air Base. Pitch black skies engulfed us with mountains everywhere. I put my faith in the lead helicopter, did my best to avoid getting vertigo, and followed their red and green position lights to Osan Air Base.

That didn't go too badly. Another day, another dollar.

Flying filled my days with incredible adventure. When not working, however, I found little to do that didn't involve drinking, and as a result, found myself partying most nights. One night, I split my forehead open after unsuccessfully attempting a backflip in some bar. Another night, I tripped over my boots when getting out of bed in the middle of the night and hit my head on a concrete wall. Something had to change.

The journey toward professionalism began with my next assignment, this time in Tucson, Arizona.

I found myself crammed into the middle seat of a Boeing 707 on what we called a cattle car flight. I listened to a 250-pound Army sergeant tell stories of pig farming in Alabama as the flight droned on forever. After what felt like a sleepless month, we landed at Travis Air Force Base in California. Fortunately, the base operated a school bus shuttle to the San Francisco Airport. From there I boarded a flight back to Wisconsin. It felt good to be home again. Without knowing it, I'd become a marginally seasoned helicopter pilot complete with the dark thrill of working in a life-or-death environment.

Before leaving South Korea, I took the U.S. Army shuttle to Seoul and ordered a Lotus Europa sports car. The agent promised it'd be delivered to Chicago. In reality, Cleveland became the vehicle off-load point. My dad and brother flew there and cleared the car through Port Customs, found a couple gallons of gasoline, and drove it to Wisconsin. I never did get all the details of their adventure but know it involved a lot more than simply filling the car with gas and hitting the highway.

My brother and sister drove it to Tucson. I'd flown ahead and moved into the townhouse of another helicopter buddy and previous roommate from Ogden, Utah. Cory Babbit had been assigned to Davis-Monthan Air Force Base immediately after completing flight training and now owned the bungalow. We'd be roommates once again.

Chapter 11

… Pilots should be brave so they won't get scared if it's foggy and they can't see, or if a wing or motor falls off.
– Fifth-grade student at Jefferson School, Beaufort, S.C.

MY NEW JOB IN TUCSON WITH THE 100TH Strategic Reconnaissance Wing added an unusual twist to flying. It included sensitive and dangerous missions. The unit consisted of two distinct groups, one of which supported high-altitude U-2 reconnaissance aircraft operations. These pilots flew lengthy missions in the U-2 and flew shorter proficiency flights in sleek T-38 jet aircraft. My half of the Wing released reconnaissance drones from under the wings of DC-130 aircraft and used helicopters to snag them in mid-air as they parachuted back to Earth. We deployed a lot. The DC-130s flew out of Vietnam and Korea. Our helicopter operations launched out of Nakhon Phanom Royal Thai Air Force Base in northeast Thailand, which we simply called NKP, and my old stomping grounds, Osan Air Base in South Korea.

In my quest to establish a more professional footing, I joined the Base Honor Guard, a volunteer organization that typically attracted only enlisted troops. I figured it couldn't hurt to have a Lieutenant join them for six months. After marching in holiday parades and leading several official ceremonies, I gained an appreciation for Air Force pomp and circumstance. Of more immediate benefit, I acquired a penchant for keeping my uniforms perfectly tailored and adorned.

Another program surfaced that I imagined could also enhance my overall development plan. The Additional Duty – Strategic Air Command program provided several months of maintenance immersion and culminated with the award of an entry-level maintenance officer specialty code. This came in handy months later, as it became a qualifying requirement for functional test-flight pilots.

My primary focus centered on learning to catch drones and sling-load them to a recovery base. New aircraft systems expanded my knowledge base and unique flying skills soon became routine.

The drone recovery operation represented hands-down, the most dangerous thing I'd done in the air. The entire process sounded routine in the pre-mission briefings, but in reality, the margin for error remained perilously thin.

DC-130E (although this is a DC-130A model) with an AQM-34L drone attached.

DC-130s carried two drones, one under each wing. Most of the missions involved four-thousand-pound Ryan AQM-34L drones flying preplanned low-level routes at five hundred miles per hour. They'd click snapshots of enemy missile and anti-aircraft artillery sites and would eventually climb to twenty-five thousand feet, fly to a recovery location, and parachute toward a waiting CH-3 helicopter. During training, four-thousand-pound concrete-filled orange canisters replaced the actual drones while using the same parachute system.

The drone recovery sequence starts at 10,000 feet altitude.

The two-parachute system made mid-air recoveries possible. A huge, one-hundred-foot diameter chute did most of the work. A smaller, twenty-five-foot diameter parachute deployed above it and served as our target. We'd initiate the recovery by climbing to ten thousand feet and then lower two long poles out the back of our helicopter, each capped with a detachable hook. An additional grappling hook hung between the poles. As the parachutes descended past us, we aligned ourselves with them, all the time aiming at the smaller chute. Everything descended at twelve hundred feet-per-minute which nearly matched our auto-rotation, or engine-out, descent rate. On a good day, the helicopter skimmed over the smaller chute and the hooks snagged its nylon webbing. Explosive squibs then separated the big chute from everything else, a critically important element of the recovery process. If the large chute didn't separate, the helicopter crew would cut the cable attached to the hooks before being pulled out of control below the large chute. One day, a crew attempted to maintain control after the large parachute failed to separate. In addition to severely over-stressing the airframe, they came within a whisper of losing control and crashing.

CH-3E helicopter ready to snag a drone.

Snagging a drone seldom occurred as a textbook process. Winds often pushed the smaller chute toward the side of the big chute making a low pass over it nearly impossible. More insidious, air spilling out from the main chute often disrupted airflow into the smaller one, causing it to pulse up and down. Detecting this from the helicopter could be difficult without a background reference, and as a result, the smaller chute pulsing upward into the rotor blades presented a constant danger.

That's exactly what happened on my first attempted orange canister catch. At the last instant, the target chute pulsed upward, covering our entire windscreen with orange nylon. We'd hit a soft wall, the nose dipped, and then dipped some more. Disaster slapped us in the face and the time to react had passed. We found ourselves helplessly in the hands of fate for a brief instant. Nano-seconds felt like minutes and ticked by in slow motion. Then the chute slid off our nose. Blue sky returned and we abruptly bobbed back to level flight. We'd come within inches of the chute entangling itself in the rotor blades. If that had happened, we'd have surely crashed.

By the end of the year, I deployed as a mission-qualified co-pilot to Nakhon Phanom, which we referred to as NKP. A KC-135 aerial refueling aircraft dropped into Davis-Monthan Air Force Base, and we boarded it the day after Christmas, 1975.

The memory of that long return flight from Korea remained fresh in my mind. This flight would surely be better with more spacious sidewall seating. We'd be riding in a dedicated aircraft, and the flight would be divided into manageable segments. The first leg of the mission ended at March Air Force Base in California.

Nylon-mesh seating had long been the standard on military aircraft and every passenger considered it universally uncomfortable. Two alternatives for settling ourselves in the back of the aircraft included sitting on the icy-cold metal floor and playing cards, or climbing into one of the overhead racks and sleeping. The temperature at the top of the cabin felt hot, maybe eighty-five degrees. The nylon seats, as uncomfortable as they were, became our least uncomfortable alternative. A middle-of-the-night refueling stop in Hawaii lasted only two hours. Moist ocean air greeted us as we walked to an isolation room near the aircraft parking location. Before we knew it, we found ourselves airborne again.

The next long and boring flight brought us to Guam where we again remained only long enough to refuel. Mid-afternoon of the third day after leaving Tucson marked our arrival at U-Tapao Royal Thailand Air Force Base. This airfield supported all sorts of military aircraft, most notably B-52 bombers and KC-135 tankers. The Vietnam War continued in full swing, and we became a part of it. Capt Parker, SSgt McClellan, and I got rooms at base billeting. After a quick shower, McClellan and I followed Parker, who claimed to know his way around, on a local area tour. We boarded a baht bus, which resembled a pick-up truck with seating in the back, and headed for some unknown town with outdoor bars.

NKP existed on the Thai-Lao border adjacent to North Vietnam.

An hour after the bars closed, McClellan and I found ourselves sitting on a curb outside a large teakwood house while our aircraft commander said "good night" to some girl he'd met at the bar. His "good night" continued for almost an hour. We wanted to leave and find our way back to the base, but neither of us had a clue how to do it, and neither of us spoke Thai. We waited.

Early the next morning, we boarded a C-130, affectionately called Klong Hopper Airways, and rode north to NKP where we'd soon begin flying our missions under the code name Buffalo Hunter.

For the next sixty days, we caught drones and lived on an isolated base that operated on a war-time rhythm. The runway had recently been paved with concrete while the tarmac remained a connected web of pierced steel planking, sometimes called Marston Mat or more commonly, PSP. These ten-foot-long by fifteen-inch-wide steel strips came with a series of holes along the length to lighten them.

At night, an AC-130 gunship orbited above the base while surveilling its perimeter. Hooch bars hosted high-stakes poker games. I remember watching 21st Special Operations Squadron aircrew and maintainers seated at a card table in the middle of a smoke-filled tent, all wagering for a four-hundred-dollar pot. These guys looked every bit like combat veterans who flew high-risk rescue missions into North Vietnam when not playing cards. They seemed more like pirates than aircrew. Our missions felt routine compared to theirs.

One day, I heard that the Airmen's Club offered a lobster Thermador dinner for only $1.75, and it soon became a prime destination during my evening wanderings. A large T-bone steak cost the same, but in my mind, it didn't seem nearly as special as the lobster. I made a point of eating dinner there three to four times a week.

At the end of February, we made our way to Bangkok for several days before catching the Klong Hopper to U-Tapao and then a KC-135 aircraft for the trans-Pacific ride home.

Shortly after I returned from Thailand my name again appeared on two-month deployment orders, this time to Osan Air Base, South Korea. I'd be the aircraft commander.

Chapter 12

Confidence is contagious. So is lack of confidence.
– Vince Lombardi

THE OSAN OPERATION USED RYAN MODEL 147TF Combat Dawn remotely piloted vehicles. These drones had a fifteen-foot wingspan which made them much more of a challenge to handle once suspended beneath our helicopters. One recovery tested the mettle of the entire crew.

Everything up to the point of snatching the drone progressed smoothly. We saw the parachute descending toward us and our first pass seemed text-book perfect until fabric filled the hook and the webbed nylon lines slipped out of our grasp. We'd helplessly gashed a long strip along the parachute. The second hook remained intact and we tried again only to shred the parachute once again without actually snagging it.

At this point, we couldn't make additional passes over the parachute. It felt like being in a shootout with an unloaded gun. We watched as the drone splashed into the ocean and then hovered several feet above the moderately rough seas while the engineer attempted to manually snag its bridle. An advisory crackled through my headset that several Chinese vessels had been identified approaching the area. F-4 fighter jets from Osan Air Base launched to sink the drone if we couldn't pull it from the South China Sea. Worse, I'd never tried this before and knew that hovering over a featureless ocean ranked as anything but easy.

Sling-loading the drone after mid-air recovery.

Somehow, we hooked the drone on our first attempt but when we lifted it from the ocean its drogue chute wrapped around the right-side wing causing a major controllability issue. Additionally, the front cowling on that same side had been damaged and twisted outward into the wind stream. The combined effect caused the drone to constantly wifferdill to the right and then do the same to the left. Inside the cockpit, the helicopter felt nearly out of control.

I reeled the drone out to four hundred feet below us. We watched it out the side windows each time it flew to our level and then turned back downward.

I spotted an isolated island with white sandy beaches ahead and landed there to reposition the drogue chute. Hopefully, the flight mechanic could also bend the damaged panel to a better position. It wouldn't budge but we did bury the drogue chute in the white sands and hoped it'd re-inflate correctly. After we took off, the chute returned to its old position, forcing us to fight the instability for the next hour as we flew home. All the dangers eventually ran their course and before long I docked the damaged drone at the end of the runway. In the end, it amounted to just another unheralded day, but a satisfying one.

We claimed the unacknowledged honor of being the last crew deployed to Korea before that operation concluded. With the Vietnam War winding down, Thailand's operation ran its course as well. Life back in Tucson settled into a more stable routine. I upgraded to instructor-pilot and found myself flying time-consuming functional check flights.

The CH-3E didn't seem to be an overly complex machine but it did have a few complex systems. I felt empowered by knowing its inner workings and its limitations so well. In aviation, systems knowledge is invaluable.

With the closure of overseas operations, our drone catches mostly happened at Fort Huachuca along the Mexican border or Gila Bend to the northwest. The flight to and from Gila Bend took a little over an hour, and I quickly lost interest in buzzing saguaro cacti and jackrabbits. When one of the flight mechanics discovered that our high-frequency radio could be tuned to the CB channels used by the truckers we tuned in and talked with them as they hauled goods between Yuma and Phoenix. On at least one occasion, we flew next to the truck's cab and waved to the guy on the other end of our conversation. Those moments always made me proud to be serving the country just like the truck driver's sacrifice in keeping our nation supplied with whatever goods he carried.

Another sunny, hot day. I sat in the cockpit, ready to fly a four-hour proficiency flight above our local desert. The first hour or two would hold my undivided focus before the flying became more routine. As it turned out, things started on a high note and got more interesting as time wore on.

Ten minutes before our departure, a U-2 took off and began climbing toward the stratosphere. Command Post called.

"Are you able to support a search mission for one of the U-2's pogos?"

The pogo assembly included a wheel attached to a spring-steel rod that slid into place under each U-2 wingtip. When the U-2 rotated for take-off, the rod/wheel assembly fell free to be retrieved by a launch support team.

Command Post clarified.

"The pilot reported that it departed his wingtip five miles from the airport at an altitude of five thousand feet."

We decided on a search pattern and began slowly flying back and forth at approximately fifty feet altitude. We never did find the pogo but we did find a body lying prone in the sand. After we landed in the desert, the co-pilot grabbed a first-aid kit and approached the corpse. He came running back to advise us that he'd discovered a dead female. After alerting the Command Post controller, he stammered, hemmed, and hawed.

"Did it appear ... do you think ... you know, could she have been struck in the head by a falling object?"

"Nope," I replied, "I think your pogo hit something else."

Before long the County Sheriff led a string of flashing red lights along nearby Interstate 10. We guided them into the desert by hover-taxiing back to the scene of the crime.

I'd moved onto the base and drifted apart from my friend Cory. He partied with a different group and I'd settled down quite a bit. Unbeknownst to me, medical issues impacted his life quite a bit and he always seemed to be elsewhere when I stopped by. I hadn't immediately known about his diagnosis of having an aggressive form of cancer. Within a year, he became bedridden, and a year later, he passed away at the youthful age of twenty-five.

Once I became aware of his terrible situation, my feelings seemed confused. How could I switch from feeling terrible for him to feeling normal for everything else? I didn't understand his pain even though I hurt for him inside. Again, death did not mix well in my mind. I promised to make the most of every day. To acknowledge the good in those around me and to know that life is little more than a fleeting firefly in the night. I miss Cory.

This assignment in Tucson, more than any other, transformed me from a carefree, somewhat undisciplined youth into a fun-loving professional who took pride in himself and the Air Force.

A bit of good luck drifted in the air. My progression into fixed-wing conversion training would occur almost a year early. In this one case, my time for reassignment coincided with a hard-to-fill vacancy for conversion training. I packed my bags and headed to Big Spring, Texas.

Chapter 13

... Pilots don't need much school. They just have to learn to read numbers so they can read their instruments. I guess they should be able to read a road map, too.
– A fifth-grade student at Jefferson School, Beaufort, S.C.

I'M SURE THERE MUST HAVE BEEN ONE PERSON on the planet who liked Big Spring, Texas, and I also suspect that person needs to have his head examined. This small west Texas crossroads consisted of the Cosden Petroleum Corporation, which stunk up the place refining gasoline, jet fuel, asphalt, synthetic plastics, and other petrochemicals. A single restaurant and gas station defined Main Street. Oh, and Webb Air Force Base existed on the outskirts of town. It contained many more buildings and housed seventy-five percent of the area's population.

Cessna T-37B Tweet. I flew 60 hours in this little beast.

I hoped to endure a short course in the twin-engine T-37 Tweet and a full course in the much faster Northrup T-38A Talon in Big Spring. On a positive note, few distractions existed within a hundred miles, and flight training did spice up the miserable location with its challenging one-year syllabus.

Vivid first-flight memories persist. Flipping inverted the first time, eyes wide, fists tightened slightly. It felt unnatural with vastly greater pressures than any roller-coaster. I'd broken loose from my attachment to the earth. A sense of unbridled freedom filled my veins. Then we banked and turned 180 degrees at a thousand feet above the runway. Sixty degrees of bank felt more like ninety. Two Gs pressed me against the seat. The dichotomous thought flashed, "Is this the greatest feeling ever … or should I throw up?"

Northrup T-38A Talon is a true challenge flying an inverted 4-ship at .98 mach.

The T-38A oozed power. Take-off. Gear up. Make the five-mile radio call. It happened within seconds. Its 180 knots approach speed exceeded 200 miles per hour. It became more challenging with each flight. Old and pilot-unfriendly avionics made the instrument check-ride in this aircraft seem particularly difficult because the margin for error remained so narrow. Happiness prevailed once I passed that ride. The speed and power and the time spent pointed every which way but straight and level, elevated flying to a new level.

The 78th Flying Training Wing also taught Iranian student exchange pilots how to fly. These guys seemed to be a mixed bag of well-to-do kids from powerful families. I played soccer with them each weekend, growing to admire many while finding disappointment in others. A few stubborn and entitled Iranians stood in sharp contrast to their modest fun-loving Iranian classmates. Most drove Ford or Chevy muscle cars, and all loved playing soccer. Being a pilot attracted different candidates from different countries. I found my way into the skies from an average background. These young men came from universally well-to-do families. Average Iranians would never find the same opportunity.

The T-37 seemed by far to be more fun to fly. It provided a real sense of rolling and pitching movement. The first time my instructor banked sixty degrees and pulled two Gs, my stomach tangled itself between my knees and I felt strangely uneasy. After that first time, the feeling never returned because I knew what to expect. The T-38 provided its own set of thrills, like accelerating on take-off while pressing my body against the back of the seat. By the time I flipped the gear handle to the "up" position, we'd have flown nearly five miles from the airfield. This called for a major mental adjustment. I needed to organize my thoughts before getting to the runway and somehow figure out how to think faster. Each sortie represented a million-dollar ride that cost me nothing beyond blood, sweat, and tears. I loved it.

Capt Jim Beaubien, my first T-38 instructor, impressed me as a quiet-spoken guy from Ponca City, Oklahoma. He made a point to be gracious in his criticism as he taught me valuable techniques. I didn't realize he'd been awarded the

Silver Star (three times) and the Distinguished Flying Cross for valor in Vietnam. Unfortunately, our relationship didn't last long as he encountered a medical issue that grounded him indefinitely.

Because I'd flown one training mission with the Squadron Commander, Col Art Burer, I became his full-time student. This at first seemed like a curse I'd have to endure as Col Burer seemed to be a no-nonsense officer. As time wore on, I found the experience to be incredibly rewarding. Col Burer happened to be a great pilot who let me struggle just enough before interjecting himself.

"Mallon, stop breathing all our oxygen," he'd comment through his oxygen mask.

When I first heard his suggestion, I realized I'd become overly focused on holding position as number three in a four-ship formation while upside down at .98 mach. At that incredible speed, every twitch on the controls bounced our airplane noticeably in relationship to the others. I'd almost hyperventilated, almost.

Col Burer became a flying father figure to me, and I came to enjoy our time together even though the times came in short snippets and passed too quickly. He'd been a Vietnam Prisoner of War for eight years, from 1965 through 1973 and he'd been released only two years earlier. Col Burer could be tough and gentle at the same time. He demanded excellence, yet tolerated my learning. I'd remember these traits and assimilate them into my bag of leadership values.

I'd taken off on my first solo flight when the air traffic controller announced that my planned training area had been closed and he then redirected me to another, seldom-used location. The change required some sort of quick visualization of which direction I needed to point the jet.

Things happened fast, but miraculously I arrived at my area without violating anyone else's assigned space. Before I landed, the aircraft radio failed and I needed to follow light signals from the tower before taxiing to parking. It couldn't have gotten much worse for a first flight ... yet I'd survived.

Getting upside down in what felt like a supersonic glass hotdog introduced another abnormal sensation. Performing a loop provided an incredible perspective on life in the sky. I pointed the aircraft nose forty-five degrees toward the earth and waited while the plane accelerated to 450 kts airspeed. Then I eased back on the stick and zoomed to 10,000 feet while flying upside down and continuing until the nose pointed to a vertical descent – like riding a lawn dart and watching the oil fields below get bigger and bigger. Now, that defined fun!

One day I called the 349th Strategic Reconnaissance Squadron Deputy Commander and asked about assignment potential as a DC-130 pilot. The idea must have resonated as that's exactly what happened. I'd soon be off to Little Rock Air Force Base to learn the intricacies of flying C-130s and then back to Tucson. Before long, I found myself fully qualified as a DC-130 copilot at my old stomping grounds, Davis-Monthan Air Force Base.

Chapter 14

The propeller is just a big fan in front of the plane used to keep the pilot cool. When it stops, you can actually watch the pilot start sweating.
– Unknown

I LEARNED TO FLY ALL OVER AGAIN. THE aerodynamics seemed pretty much the same, but all the other stuff changed, including international regulations, complex aircraft systems, and more detailed mission planning. The pilots in my new unit included Capt Steve Fleming who'd be my primary instructor until I became a functioning co-pilot. Steve later found himself at Desert One in Iran during Operation Eagle Claw. He lived life at a laid-back and easygoing pace. Yet he knew the aircraft inside out and possessed incredible airborne situational awareness. He represented everything I valued in a pilot, and I feel fortunate to have learned from him.

Three others who later followed paths into the world of special operations included Capts Jack Nimo, Bill Ross, and big John Ozlins. At the time I only knew that we'd become highly proficient aviators. Looking back, quite a few became unheralded national heroes.

One night during the heat of July, we departed Tucson and headed for Roosevelt Roads Naval Station, Puerto Rico. Another young Captain occupied the left seat and I sat in the right one. After droning across Texas and the Gulf of Mexico we dropped into Miami's Homestead Air Force Base for fuel. Midnight and sticky hot, lightning flashed over the Atlantic and foretold of a challenging ride ahead. Off we went.

We leveled off, turned on the autopilot, kicked back, and secured a large bucket of Kentucky Fried Chicken on the throttle quadrant. Moderate turbulence kept us alert between the Nav's heading changes. Then a large whitish blob appeared on our radar screen.

"Nav, either we're headed into a massive storm or we're about to overfly someone's country."

Then, from the nav station.

"Oh...stand by...come to a heading of north...we just entered Dominican Republic airspace."

We now knew where we were, at least for the time being. An hour later and after many, many turns to avoid thunderstorms, our navigation radio continued its unsuccessful scans for Borinquen VOR. Borinquen marked the westernmost point of Puerto Rico and once we could identify it we'd be home-free. We hadn't been in radio contact with anyone for hours.

I contacted Puerto Rico Radio and requested what we called a Direction Finding or DF steer. Before getting a DF steer, one of our navaids suddenly locked onto Borinquen. Thank goodness. The aviation gods must have nodded in our favor because no one knew exactly how to set the radios for a DF steer. The process consisted of fairly simple steps, requiring us to make an extended radio broadcast while the ground controller worked his magic to determine the origin of the signal.

The navigator proceeded to eat what remained of our chicken. He must have been more stressed than we'd realized. The sun peeked out from the horizon as we landed. We didn't run out of fuel. We hadn't been struck by lightning. We somehow found Puerto Rico, and, we ate some pretty good chicken along the way. This had all the makings of another memorable trip.

Not all the missions tipped the scales toward "fun." We participated in several Red Flag missions that centered operations north of Nellis Air Force Base in Las Vegas. We'd fly directly from Tucson, execute our part of the mission, and then turn around and fly home. No gambling for us.

Unfortunately, these missions generated a ton of annoying radio chatter. In addition to the aircraft intercom supporting eight to ten crewmembers, two active UHF radios, a VHF radio, an FM radio, and an HF radio needed monitoring. It became common to monitor or communicate via all five radios, a mentally draining experience.

We found ourselves occasionally plagued with unusual drone malfunctions. One day, a launched drone suddenly blocked all control signals and made a beeline for the middle of the highly classified Area 51 where it crashed. Controllers directed the DC-130 aircrew to immediately land at Nellis Air Force Base. We saw them again about a week later. They wouldn't talk about their experience.

Several months later, our Group Commander, Col Jim Witzel, received a call from the Pentagon. A Los Angeles Times reporter had been driving along Interstate 10 toward Los Angeles when he spotted a strange vehicle parachuting to a spot near the side of the highway. He pulled over.

The Group Commander related his conversation to me.

"He left two sets of footprints in the desert sand. The first set appeared to be closely spaced as he approached the drone. The second set stretched much farther apart as he fled back to his car. He'd read the DANGER – RADIOACTIVE warning label and thought it must have been a nuclear-tipped cruise missile."

Fortunately, he related the story to his editor before writing it. The editor called the Pentagon and asked if the military had lost one of their cruise missiles – one that might have been headed toward Los Angeles.

The drone had lost connectivity with the DC-130, flew in circles until it reached recovery mode, then climbed to 25,000 feet, and headed west until running out of fuel.

The Group Director of Operations almost crashed my aircraft one day while flying an approach into Kirtland Air Force Base in Albuquerque, New Mexico. We found ourselves inside a snowstorm. Our approach path to Kirtland's runway initially looked good. Then the aircraft slipped below the glidepath. No correction.

"Below glide path," I advised.

We broke out of the clouds. Sequential flashing lights.

"Runway in sight."

The Rio Grande River basin flowed between us and the airport and created the illusion of our aircraft being high on the glide slope, just the opposite of our situation. We descended farther, and farther below the glideslope. I advised him with an increasing urgency. The runway disappeared as we descended into the Rio Grande Valley and found ourselves below the level of the runway. I heard a panicked comment from the tower controller as I slammed my hand over the commander's hand on the throttles and pushed them to full power. The runway came back into view. We landed. Silence.

I debriefed the DO separately and then debriefed the rest of the crew for not speaking up. I'd found my limits, and almost felt the consequence of exceeding them. That approach marked a significant change in how I flew. It represented a line in the sand that under no circumstance would I cross. Getting close to the line warranted extreme caution, crossing it represented an unforgivable mistake.

Chapter 15

No one has a life where everything that happened was good. I think the thing that made life good for me is that I never looked back. I've always been positive, no matter what happened.
– Wilma Rudolph

DURING MY LAST YEAR IN TUCSON, I PURSUED a master's degree in business administration. It represented an unspoken promotional requirement that I'd need if I decided to remain in the Air Force. It'd also serve me well if I explored the civilian market. Getting it, however, wouldn't be easy.

The school only offered a couple of courses each month and I needed thirteen specific ones. To do this fast, I'd take a class each month, and in months when I couldn't find a specific class available in Tucson, I'd travel to Luke Air Force Base in Phoenix or Fort Huachuca along the Mexican border. A grueling year later, I finished. The final, comprehensive exam spanned two days. Day one covered multiple-choice questions while day two involved writing a comprehensive case study.

How could I have gotten it so wrong and still passed?

I analyzed sales data and developed a market expansion plan for Vlasic Pickles, Inc. I recommended limiting production to approximately twelve varieties and expanding regionally to test the waters before going national. It seemed conservative and prudent. That night I relaxed with a can of beer and a jar of kosher dill pickles.

"Damn, these are Vlasics. Why are they available in Arizona?"

I read the label to discover they produced over a hundred varieties nationally. Oh, oh. Solid analysis and logical reasoning ... and the professor probably never read a Vlasic label.

Our military unit began deactivating in the months ahead. I'd been assigned to fly the world's largest aircraft, the giant C-5 Galaxy, affectionately called Fat Albert. The decision wore on me, I loved the idea of flying this aircraft around the globe. It'd provide worthy missions and it'd lead to an airline pilot job if I wanted. But I'd become energized by the business world. It represented a place where profit and loss measured business success, where expenses mattered. Sure, government work included fiscal restraints, but with different consequences. Rather than accept the C-5 assignment, I submitted "7-day option" paperwork and separated from the Air Force.

An emerging paper-products company called Green Bay Packaging had developed an upper-level management training program after forecasting a need for additional plant managers. They began searching for candidates with a business background and management experience. In many ways, I looked like the perfect candidate and reported for work two weeks later.

Manufacturing corrugated board had always been an invisible industry to me even though I grew up in a community whose top five companies did just that. My first assignment took me to Arkansas where I rented a car and drove to the sleepy town of Morrilton. A forest manager met me the next morning, and we explored a portion of the company's 250,000 acres of sustainable forest. Paper-producing trees required eight years of growth before harvesting and reforestation occurred. Traipsing about the forest felt natural. Seeing it being managed added a new dimension. The job seemed like a good one.

The company operated an old rural sawmill with incredibly precise auto-programmed saw blades. Its staff of less than twenty included three of the most beautiful women I'd ever seen. One had been a top runner-up for Miss Arkansas.

Another much larger facility produced Kraft paper. Here, workers transformed wood chips into a rough fluted sheet that formed the middle of a corrugated sheet. We never called it cardboard. After all, cardboard didn't have a fluted center. Huge rolls of this paper rode on trains to Green Bay.

As much as I wanted to stay and work in Arkansas, the training forced me back to Green Bay. I trained by day and tinkered on cars at night.

Returning to Green Bay full-time felt like a more permanent lifestyle. The daytime work hours and the sense that I'd remain in Greem Bay for the foreseeable future allowed me to tinker with bigger personal projects. I bought an aging British-made MGB. This time I removed the engine and transmission and had both rebuilt. Eventually, I got it all together again and drove it for several months before selling it. In the process, I learned a lot about troubleshooting auto issues. Management training and the auto rebuild project kept life interesting.

During the next year, I designed boxes that cradled things like glass coffee pots and odd-shaped appliances. The Safety Compliance department drop-tested everything and when our designs passed, they moved into production. I worked as a shift foreman on the huge corrugated board production machines. These ran the length of a football field with huge rolls of different thickness paper combining top, bottom, and corrugated fluting into a continuous composite sheet. The single strand ran through felt drying belts before being cut, creased, and chopped into finished sheets. I watched as six-foot-tall men lost forty pounds in their first week. Skinny kids persevered and kept going. The work environment took its toll on everyone, brutal, hot, and very humid.

Now and again, a worker would go a bit crazy. One guy attacked a fellow worker with a hammer, while another worker commandeered a forklift and tried to run down a senior foreman.

I smelled like wet paper at the end of every shift. Nonetheless, I liked the work.

In some ways, I remained naive and it soon caught up to me. One night while attending an out-of-town training seminar, one of the young Milwaukee salesmen asked about my position.

"… so where are you going to eventually work?"

I didn't know exactly, so I explained the management program as I understood it.

"I'm in training. The plan is to gain exposure to all aspects of the company so that I can someday become a plant manager."

In the military, this explanation would have been perfectly normal, but it didn't sit well with the salesman. His long-term aspirations included becoming a plant manager. I'd shown up without experience and appeared ready to steal his dream.

Later that week, the plant manager, who also headed the sales force, called me to his office. The corporate manager with oversight for my training already occupied one of two chairs. This didn't feel good. As I recall, I got ripped. I know the hair on the back of my neck stiffened.

Where did all of this hate come from?

I went back to my desk in Estimating wondering what had just happened.

This isn't going to work.

Three days later, as if the Air Force spied on my life, I received a letter requesting a possible return to active duty. A significant pilot shortfall needed resolution and my support would be appreciated.

This "pilot shortage" had been a recurring problem for years. The time required to establish a pilot training pipeline never seemed to match budgetary cycles. This historical imbalance produced too many pilots followed several years later by too few pilots. Once again, timing defined everything.

Within the month, I parted ways with Green Bay Packaging and pointed my nose back toward Little Rock Air Force Base. I still hurt from the recent tongue-lashing but never looked back. I learned an important lesson, to be more sensitive to the motivations of others and to become less blunt about things in general.

Capt Lenny Lake at the Military Personnel Center asked whether I'd prefer an assignment to Pope Air Force Base in North Carolina, Little Rock AFB in Arkansas, or Dyess AFB in Abilene, Texas.

"I've never been assigned to the East Coast, so how about Pope?" I replied.

"I'm so sorry, it's no longer available … blah, blah, blah."

"Okay. Well, Little Rock isn't too far from Wisconsin. How about Little Rock?"

"The slot there just got filled … blah, blah, blah."

"Okay, I've been thinking about Dyess all along."

Capt Lake's attempts to deliver physical orders to Green Bay had about as much success as shooting arrows at a passing bird. On the Friday before my Little Rock C-130 requalification start date, he dictated verbal orders over the phone. A week later numerous sets of orders started arriving in the mail.

Late in the afternoon on the day after receiving Lenny's verbal orders, I approached Little Rock Air Force Base's main gate. I rolled down the window.

"I don't have military ID … Ugh, no uniforms … No, I don't have a vehicle sticker … Can't you see I'm traveling on verbal orders."

"Sir, you'll have to go to the office."

Somehow, I received a week-long visitor's pass before driving to the billeting office where a middle-aged roadblock looked me in the face.

"May I have a copy of your orders?"

Normally, without orders, the billeting staff wouldn't talk to someone wanting a room. I had untrimmed hair and a story about verbal orders.

"Please call Capt Lenny Lake. He's the one who ordered me here. He can explain. Besides, my class starts Monday morning." And that soon became my next problem ...

The receptionist handed me a room key, and two mornings later I started looking for the correct classroom. Package after package of orders began showing up, and eventually I had a new ID, uniforms, flight gear, and any number of other required items.

I found myself back in the Air Force and ready to resume flying.

Chapter 16

You can observe a lot by just watching.
– Yogi Berra

THREE FLYING SQUADRONS AT Dyess Air Force Base comprised the 463rd Tactical Airlift Wing. I'd been assigned to the 774th Tactical Airlift Squadron. It felt good to belong to a like-minded group. Better yet, I'd be flying all sorts of mainstream missions.

Following a relatively quick aircraft commander checkout, I either flew or scheduled others to fly. Days passed quickly. I became part of a quirky Crew Coordination staff that gained notoriety when Maj Howie Allen joined Capt Ben Fallin and me to manage exercise deployments. We'd work sixteen-hour shifts juggling crewmember combinations against thousands of qualifying details. Fallin projected a serious, professional demeanor. Allen seemed the reincarnation of comedian Buddy Hacket – chubby, light-hearted, and outrageously funny. And me? At this point, I amounted to just another pilot.

Night tactical training missions routinely consisted of six aircraft. One night, Allen, Fallin, and I commanded separate aircraft in the formation. But before we could taxi to the runway, the other three planes never started their engines due to maintenance issues. Howie called the Command Post to update the formation positions for each of the three routes we'd fly.

"On the first route, it'll be Allen number one, Fallin number two, and Mallon number three ... Wait, ah ... make that Allen, Mallon, and Fallin. Airdrop two ... Mallon one, Allen two, Fallin three. Drop three, Fallin, Mallon, Allen ... no, ah, wait ... on two put Mallon, Fallin, Allen, and on three try Fallin, Allen, then Mallon."

Muffled laughs crackled across multiple radios, including Ground Control, who must have monitored the comical exchange on Command Post's frequency.

A long pause ensued.

"Copy," Command Post responded.

An exclusive professional organization of military pilots called The Order of Daedalians reached out to me and I joined. This fraternal group always hosted don't-miss-it monthly meetings. I escorted Tex Hill to one of our meetings and knew him as the Flying Tigers' squadron leader of the American Volunteer Group in Burma. Actor John Wayne played him in the movie *The Flying Tigers*. Tex became a triple ace and a man who in his 70s could handle his whiskey. I also escorted Gabby Gabreski, another WWII ace. He briefed our small group on his flying exploits in the European Theater. I came to feel a part of this colorful heritage as flying now identified my profession, one that created heroes and took young lives.

Check-rides held value in measuring average pilots as the experience motivated them to study and held them to acceptable standards. But being simply average didn't fit my definition of the "professional" category. Being great did that, and I wanted to be a professional. It sunk in.

WALK RUN FLY

A Marine Corps Reserve training weekend set the tone for missions during the years that followed. Early one Saturday morning, ten of our C-130s scattered to the far reaches of the U.S. I flew to Naval Air Station Glenview on the north side of Chicago. Our IFF/SIF, which provides airspace controllers with a data-filled blip on their scope, failed as we entered Chicago O'Hare's approach-control airspace. Busy controllers didn't sound happy until we landed. The system began working at that point so we continued the mission only to have it fail again on departure. Controllers hounded us repeatedly until we flew a hundred miles west of Chicago. Our destination – a dirt strip in the desert near Twenty-nine Palms, California. From there we'd fly to Norton Air Force Base near Los Angeles and spend the night.

Aside from the IFF/SIF failure, the mission progressed smoothly until we attempted a desert landing in the dark of night. It took the aircraft commander three attempts to properly line up the runway before crunching our plane onto its dirt strip. As we departed for Norton AFB, our remaining fuel consisted of mostly fumes. For the only time in my life, I declared "Emergency Fuel." We'd either land at Norton or crash, as no other landing options existed. All the fuel low-level lights illuminated and we felt eminently close to flaming out engines. A deep breath, power back, we made it.

The Utility Hydraulic System never felt too complex, but you'd never know it from looking at it.

Each week, our Chief of Training officer tasked a young co-pilot to research a complicated aircraft system and explain it during Friday's ground training session. 1st Lt Dave Scott volunteered to explain the prop housing. This kluge of speeder springs and fly-weights would put Rube Goldberg to shame. Scott explained the entire system using simple, understandable analogies. Forty years later I still remember his briefing. Nothing ever seemed too complex, although the prop housing came close. I set a goal to understand systems to the same extent that Dave understood them. He impressed me as a professional.

Exercise Red Flag brought together aircraft from throughout the Air Force to Las Vegas, Nevada, where their aircrews trained in an extremely realistic combat environment. We flew four of our C-130s to Nellis Air Force Base to participate in one such week-long exercise. Two vans transported us between our run-down hotel and the airport. The squadron commander, Lt Col Bill Orellana, drove a rental car. We relaxed at the blackjack tables, drank complimentary drinks, and generally had a good time on the first night. We never heard the commotion in the parking lot. In the morning, the commander noticed multiple bullet holes in his car. Apparently, there'd been a shoot-out and his car became one of the victims. We found the incident more funny than troubling and had mostly forgotten it by the end of the day.

My first exposure to gambling's dark side intensified as the week progressed. I'd win a little and then lose more. The cycle repeated itself. I made a cash withdrawal on my credit card, and then a second. I'd lost six hundred dollars during the week. Not a crippling amount, but far more than I'd intended to spend.

I haven't gambled since. I harbor no ill thoughts toward those who love to wager their money. But for me, losing doesn't sit well, especially when I have minimal control over the outcome.

At the beginning of April each year, our squadron flew sixteen aircraft across the North Atlantic to RAF Mildenhall in East Anglia, England. We spent the next two months augmenting the European airlift. Destinations felt exotic, mission planning became a bit more complex, and enroute radio calls often sounded cryptic. We flew to all the normal destinations like Madrid, Ramstein, Frankfurt, Aviano, Athens, Chania on the island of Crete, and Incirlik in Turkey. Other, lesser-known destinations popped up each week. We comprised the Bravo Squadron and we made memories to last a lifetime.

Flying across the North Atlantic, especially at night, brought with it incredible jaw-dropping views the average person will never experience. The aurora Borealis, when seen from 25,000 feet, offers an ethereal experience almost beyond words. Solar winds reacting with the earth's magnetosphere create million-mile splashes of greenish, purple, and red colors. The effect is mesmerizing. Live, pulsing colors danced before us for hours.

Our navigator explained the Van Allen belt, named after the American physicist James Van Allen who discovered it. These areas consist of protons, electrons, and heavier ions, all imprisoned within the Earth's magnetic field. Solar winds cause them to move, collide with each other, and as a result, emit light.

Another startling view grabbed my focus, the enormous icebergs appearing below us. The moon illuminated their icy-white mass against the inky black waters. If only I'd experienced this before taking high school science classes. Why couldn't I have had more curiosity then? It seems so insatiable now.

Chapter 17

Airspeed, altitude, and brains. Two are always needed to successfully complete the flight.
– Unknown

FLYING DIDN'T ALWAYS GENERATE CHEERY and bright feelings. The year before my arrival, the unit lost a six-man aircrew and a dozen passengers when their C-130 exploded and crashed fifteen miles short of Incirlik Air Base. Some suspected rebels downed the aircraft. No one knew for sure.

Two years later, in 1982, another of our aircraft crashed in Turkey's remote north-central mountains. An engine mounting bolt hadn't been reinstalled after maintenance. The number four engine developed a harmonic vibration and moments later separated from the wing, causing the number three engine to fail. The aircraft yawed to the right and the wing structure failed, folded upward, and broke free. Twenty-eight airmen died in the crash.

I landed at an austere hard-to-find airport a month later to extract the recovery team. Towering mountains on all sides made the approach perilous. We avoided clouds while flying a descending flight path down a winding gorge that opened onto a slightly wider plain. I spotted the runway at the end of the open area.

Those who boarded the plane wore clothes covered with frozen mud and snow. Chilling temps. Remote. Isolated. Darkness for the C-130 community.

We departed and initiated a corkscrew climb through an overcast cloud deck while hoping to get above the snow-capped mountains. Immediately after entering the clouds the instrument panel suddenly flashed with off flags for attitude, heading, and bearing pointers.

If I descend back down to clear skies and land, we'll be forced to stay at this god-forsaken airfield indefinitely. If I climb, we're gonna have issues, like keeping ourselves right-side up and clear of terrain. All the engines look good. Keep climbing.

I flew needle, ball, and airspeed until breaking free of the clouds. We entered the upper world of sunshine and blue skies. After several minutes of troubleshooting, we discovered the Radio Control circuit breaker to have failed. This darned single-point-of-failure breaker seemed to control all of our now-failed instrument panel gauges. Nonetheless, we'd make due with our remaining systems and find our way back to Incirlik. None of our navaid receivers worked and only a backup radio seemed to connect with controllers. With a bit of effort, we found our way home.

Many considered the Mildenhall Air Feat to be one of England's premier airshows. I put myself on standby aircrew duty to allow those who'd flown during the week the time to relax and drink while mingling with thousands of British aviation fanatics. It'd be highly unlikely that a standby crew would be tasked to fly, especially with a major airshow clogging up the airfield. Wrong.

We received a tasking to depart as soon as possible for Incirlik, Turkey. Our flight path would take us across the English Channel, through France and Italy, and into Athens, Greece. We'd refuel as quickly as possible and then proceed on to Incirlik. With more than an ounce of luck, I found everyone on the standby crew, except the engineer. More luck. An available engineer answered the phone and I tagged him to fly the mission. We'd simply deliver the aircraft and fly back on whatever available airlift we could find.

Since we'd be departing during the flight demonstration portion of the Air Feat, the announcer worked us into his narrative.

"And next we have a Bravo Squadron aircrew responding to a very important short-notice tasking …"

I pulled back on the yoke, then pushed forward to maintain a hundred-foot altitude.

"Gear up … flaps up."

As we passed crowd-center I pulled up thirty-five degrees and held it until the airspeed screamed, "Level off!"

The original standby engineer stood next to our squadron commander in a state of mild shock as he watched his crew depart without him.

We needed more wholesome nighttime entertainment while in Mildenhall. Movies came to mind. Outdoor movies with popcorn and beer. The vision materialized easily, however, making it happen became a bit more complicated. I attended a short course on the operation of audio/visual equipment, and once certified, I gained permission to sign out a 16mm projector. I quickly reserved one for the duration of our deployment. I also coordinated the checkout of military historical films.

The films could only be checked out from Ramstein Air Base in Germany. That's where all the feature-length movies existed. Before long I had co-pilots checking out and later returning weekly feature films.

We bought a popcorn popper, hung a large bedsheet from third-floor windows, and strung an extension cord to the middle of the parking lot. Business boomed ... until the General's wife complained about all the noise on Friday nights.

Bravo Squadron brought a healthy combination of European flying experience, after-hours frolicking, and occasional insanity. Unfortunately, it also held the icy hand of death.

Chapter 18

The bad news is time flies. The good news is you're the pilot.
– Michael Althsuler.

I'D BEEN LUCKY. I'D NEVER SHUT DOWN TWO engines on the same flight. Unfortunately, my luck changed.

Each year the Wing Commander sponsored a civic leaders' tour of Bravo Squadron operations throughout Europe. Not exactly a boondoggle, but a good trip. Each location highlighted our commitment to maintaining NATO's alliance. The associated flights droned on for hours, but led to incredible on-ground experiences. I'd been selected to be the aircraft commander for one such mission. A promising young captain who'd spent his recent past commanding a desk in the Wing's Executive Office would be my co-pilot. TSgt Frank Venditti, a tough-as-nails flight engineer who knew the aircraft inside out, would keep us out of trouble. I liked and trusted him. In addition to eight civilians, the entourage included Col Butterfield, the Wing Commander, Col Payne, the Director of Operations, and Capt Dave Scott, Chief of Standardization and Evaluation. No pressure to do things correctly on this one …

Abilene, Texas, disappeared behind us as I pointed the nose toward Goose Bay, Labrador. Throughout the climb, level-off, and initial cruise, we pushed through clear skies amid good conversation. Hours later and somewhere over the remoteness of northern Canada, I climbed out of the seat to stretch my legs in the cargo compartment.

I returned to find one of the city fathers occupying my seat. The Wing Commander had offered it to him in my absence. While the autopilot kept everything in order, the co-pilot unfolded a huge chart to pinpoint our exact location. His chart blocked the incredible view outside and more importantly, the instruments in front of him. We bobbed along at Flight Level 250. Airspeed, altitude, and heading all remained constant. That's when things started happening ...

We heard the number three prop change speed as it surged back and forth barely within its two percent limit. Then it became erratic. Pressure fluctuated.

"Let's keep a close eye on it."

It surged out of limits. Venditti flipped the prop control to "null." It continued surging.

"Let's shut it down."

A small boom sounded as Venditti caged the engine.

"We've got two engines out!"

The number two engine flamed out at the same time Venditti shut down the number three engine.

I pulled the civilian from my seat. Quick reactions kept the aircraft flying. I didn't have time to adjust the seat or strap in. The aircraft immediately slowed after losing half its thrust, and the autopilot's Altitude Hold function raised the nose to maintain FL250. It had already inched upward way too high. We came close to stalling. I disconnected the autopilot and pushed the nose forward. The co-pilot crumbled his chart out of the way and helped assess the overall situation while I kept the aircraft flying.

Once descending with safe flying speed, I called Toronto Center, requested a lower altitude, and declared an emergency. We all had the same puzzled thought.

"What just happened?"

After some discussion, we determined the prop synchrophasor, which at the time controlled the prop speed on the other three engines, had failed. Its last rpm spike led to the shutdown of the number three engine and also caused what we later discovered to be an inlet turbine blade failure. The sheared turbine blade destroyed the number two engine.

Trees filled the landscape for as far as we could see. No cities. No roads. We continued a slow descent toward North Bay, Ontario which happened to be along our flight path. We remained airborne for the 150 nautical miles it took to reach the runway.

"Let's restart number three."

When shutting down an engine in flight, a prop brake engages so that the prop won't continue to spin and cause undue drag. As much as we tried, we couldn't get it to disengage. We accelerated in a mild dive to 250 knots. Nothing. We then tried again while holding the starter button which added more force to drive the prop out of feather. Nothing.

Only when I flared the plane during the two-engine landing did the number three prop finally come out of feather. It idled as we taxied to parking.

We departed for Goose Bay three days later with a new engine and propeller housing installed. Over the next ten days, we flew from RAF Mildenhall north of London, across the Alps to Aviano AFB in northern Italy, then across the Aegean Sea to Athens in Greece, to Incirlik AB in Turkey, to Sigonella AB in Sicily, Torrejon AB in Madrid, and back to RAF Mildenhall. We limped our way across the North Atlantic and back to Abilene without further disruption. This is not to say we didn't encounter significant maintenance issues. We adopted the philosophy that if a component leaked, it still had fluid. Each leak prompted an evaluation. We discussed it and ultimately determined to move forward. Tough decisions.

This experience reinforced the principle that solid systems knowledge leads to better decision-making.

I checked the monthly Flying Forecast and noticed my name penciled in for a flight to Hawaii and back. The mission objective included logging a large chuck of hours before a time-phased inspection. We'd get navigator training in the process.

Why just Hawaii? Heck, if we compress downtime we can stretch the mission to Guam, Japan, and the Philippines. Now, that would get navigator training.

I presented a training plan and got it approved. Off we went ...

The second day took us eight hours into nautical nothingness west of Hawaii. GPS wouldn't be a reality for another ten years. I prayed the navigator had maintained his proficiency in using the aircraft sextant for daytime celestial readings. I'd once tried it and knew the challenge of taking precise readings. The aircraft bobbed through the air as it flew and that compromised the steady platform required for accurate readings.

An ADF beacon on Johnston Atoll served as our backup. We only needed to fly close enough to receive the signal and determine our position. Maybe atmospheric conditions dampened the signal. Maybe the ADF station had been out of commission. Whatever the case, we never did pick up the signal ... our fate rested in the navigator's hands and his Galileo-era sextant. We'd gone too far to turn back.

A speck below the aircraft nose called Kwajalein Atoll stretched into a runway surrounded by water.

"That? That's it?"

If I'd known the tiny size of our target, I'm not sure I'd have departed Hawaii. The precarious nature of long-range overwater navigation caused me to think of all those who crossed the Pacific before me. I wondered if they felt the same coldness in their stomachs. We landed.

We flew to somewhat closer airfields when back in Abilene. Bermuda offered an island experience with a sophisticated British flavor. St. Croix and St. Thomas provided a more tropical backdrop. Other airfields demanded higher technical proficiency. Toncontin Airfield in Honduras stretched for six thousand feet. The final approach descended along the contour of a mountain that ended at the threshold. A successful flight path remained approximately a hundred feet above the slope. The far end of the runway dropped off sharply for hundreds of feet into the city of Tegucigalpa. It challenged me with its tough approach. The History Channel rated it the second most extreme in the world.

An insurgency flared in neighboring El Salvador and we found ourselves delivering ammunition to Ilopango airport on several occasions. The runway featured a severe upslope at the approach end. At midfield, Trans-American Highway vehicles crossed it willy-nilly.

Our pre-mission intelligence briefings focused on clearing cows from the runway and avoiding vehicles.

"Oh, by the way, there's insurgent activity nearby and the base came under a rocket attack several days ago."

Someone issued combat helmets and flak vests, which copilots found troubling. I flashed back to memories of my time in northern Thailand during the Vietnam War. This didn't feel nearly as dangerous. Challenging, yes. Dangerous, not so much.

I blasted a recording of Wagner's Ride of the Valkyries throughout the plane as we "coasted in" over Honduras. Copilots sat on their flak vests. I became that crazy Air Cavalry commander, Lieutenant Colonel Bill Kilgore, in *Apocalypse Now*.

On another El Salvador mission, we staged the mission out of Little Rock Air Force Base. Right off the bat, our fully loaded, 175,000-pound aircraft needed a tire change. The take-off window neared and maintenance personnel found themselves without time to remove the cargo. They jacked the aircraft at its wartime weight limit. It creaked as the wheels inched off the tarmac as though the side of the airframe simply bent upward. I didn't see any big airframe cracks or fluid leaks so we started the engines and off we went. It took ten thousand feet of runway to get airborne. The Herk clawed for altitude the entire way to the Yucatan Peninsula. That's when the number three engine flamed out.

We descended and advised Havana Center in somewhat general terms of our dilemma. Shortly thereafter, the number two engine propeller surged two percent – its maximum limit. If it quit, we'd most likely keep descending right into the ocean. The flight engineer computed a service ceiling of three hundred feet, give or take a few. State Department advised us to reverse course back toward Little Rock. Too far. We flew another four hours to the nearest friendly airfield, Howard Air Base in Panama. If State preferred, we'd quietly jettison our cargo and then reverse course. Crickets…

Howard AB ground handlers moved the munitions to another C-130 and a stand-by aircrew flew it back to El Salvador. All that happened while we slept. The next day we flew back to Little Rock.

In-flight emergencies became almost routine. During one stretch, I shut down an engine on eight consecutive flights. Some seemed more or less precautionary, like Nacelle Overheats and Engine Fire indications. More serious situations appeared as well. Un-commanded throttle movement. Pressure fluctuations and oil loss.

One night while operating out of El Paso we delivered an armored personnel carrier to a dirt strip in the middle of nowhere. It'd be a heavy landing at the maximum allowable weight of 130,000 pounds. Inky skies merged seamlessly with a black desert. Only the dim glow of oil-burning pots illuminated one side of the runway.

"I've got the lights in sight."

Moments later we touched down. I stepped on the brakes. Nothing!

"There's a damned marshaller on the end of the runway. Dang, hope we don't shred him."

I pushed my toes harder, then released them.

"Emergency brakes!"

The co-pilot flipped a switch that'd give us one last-ditch application. It worked.

We could be stuck for a week. Not good. That'd negate all other landing operations ... We didn't need brakes for the takeoff, but we might need them for landing. The book required them. If we stayed here, we'd be stuck in the desert for days. El Paso had a 12,000-foot runway. That'd be plenty. I weighed the alternatives.

"Crew, we're getting out of here. Anyone have a big issue with that?"

It turned out to be a good call.

Chapter 19

Acceptance testing is anticipated with distaste, performed with reluctance, and bragged about forever.
– Anonymous

A DAY WORTHY OF CELEBRATION OCCURRED when the Air Force funded a state-of-the-art C-130H flight simulator. It represented a giant technology leap from the simplistic "blue box" Links I'd endured at Ft Rucker. The squadron identified several of us for acceptance flight testing at Binghamton, New York, the home of Singer-Link Flight Simulators. Fall colors exploded in bright yellows, reds, and browns onto an unending spread of trees. We witnessed this beauty on the day we arrived and on the day we left. In between, we lived inside Singer's production facility or inside the simulator itself. Each of our two pilot and engineer crews worked ten- to twelve-hour shifts for eight days of testing. We'd fly a four-hour mission, debrief, and then fly another one.

Each time we'd fly into Little Rock AFB, we mysteriously crashed while exactly ten miles on the final approach. An invisible spike in the terrain elevation data slapped us with an "out-of-the-blue" jolt and a flashing red screen displaying C-R-A-S-H-E-D. The repetitive experience left us a bit shell-shocked.

We tired of stressful emergencies and surprise terrain spikes by the fourth or fifth day and decided to try aileron rolls. This is a maneuver, that while technically doable in a C-130, is prohibited. In addition to over-stressing the wings, it could slosh fuel forcefully enough to rupture the wing tanks. We mastered the aileron rolls rather quickly and moved on to barrel rolls. This proved to be a mistake. We crashed several times trying to pull out of a severe nose-down attitude. Then a high-pressure hydraulic line burst, and we virtually crash-landed. Two days later, the test director informed us the system had been repaired. He also limited us to flying assigned profiles. Eventually, the acceptance tests concluded and the simulator found its way to Dyess AFB.

I participated in airshows around the country during the summer months. Every once in a while, I airdropped something or performed a maximum-effort landing and takeoff. Airshow training didn't exist and it seemed to me that practicing a routine beforehand made good sense.

Seldom did the pilot need to push the performance limits of such a big, slow aircraft. Flying near stall speed looked no different to an observer on the ground than flying faster with a comfortable safety margin. Flying too fast in a C-130 is nearly impossible. Why stress the airframe and not impress anyone while doing it? Steep bank angles in a level turn also generate unnecessary stress. Better to initiate the steep bank with the nose up and then let it fall through the horizon as I rolled out. A lapse in this conservative approach almost killed us during a practice session.

I banked and descended during a tight turn to a spot landing. Too tight, too slow. I set myself up for a classic turn-to-final stall. When the angle-of-bank gets too high and airspeed gets too low, control response fades and the aircraft is prone to flip inverted or simply mush into the ground.

I slowed to the threshold speed and maintained it. Halfway through the turn, the ailerons stopped working. We became too slow to pull back on the yoke without stalling. The windscreen filled with the overrun and grew bigger. I added full power and used the rudder pedals to level the wings. It worked. We went around. Safe. Relieved. I learned another big lesson.

"There are old pilots and there are bold pilots, but there are no old bold pilots."

I henceforth viewed airshows more conservatively.

I flew alongside incredible pilots and legendary navigators like Capt Val "Chico" Laughlin who once explained a three-mile short of target airdrop as follows.

"Well sir, in all my years of flying I've amassed an average time-over-target variation of fewer than thirty seconds. Of course, occasionally I had to sacrifice a little accuracy."

Military planners in the bowels of the Pentagon decided that special operations forces needed some form of reinforcement. An augmenting force of C-130s, C-17s, and even a C-5 would train in Special Operations Low-Level flights to blacked-out airfields. We called it SOLL II.

Assigning aircrews became very selective of necessity. They required precision flying skills and above-average airborne situational awareness. SOLL II aircrews flew without using ground-based navigation aids susceptible to enemy jamming or deception. To eliminate aircraft illumination, the engineer turned off external lights, while inside the cockpit, we stuck electrical tape over the instrument lights. A very faint green glow remained for only the most critical instruments.

The aging airborne radar, an old Sperry AN/APN-59, worked well in identifying weather but poorly when aimed lower for ground navigation. GPS remained in development and unavailable for aircraft use. Finding a blacked-out airfield without precision equipment tested the mettle of the navigator. Simply put, it constituted a very dangerous procedure.

One of our aircrews crashed short of the runway at Indian Springs Air Force Auxiliary Base. Seven servicemen in the cargo compartment burned to death in the fiery aftermath. The program continued despite the risks, and shortly thereafter I joined the adventure.

My first exposure to the world of special operations stirred a reserve of adrenaline. The flight regime demanded excellence. Missions mattered. Without realizing it, I'd become an Air Commando of sorts.

Chapter 20

Over the years, I've given myself a thousand reasons to keep running, but it always comes back to where it started. It comes down to self-satisfaction and a sense of achievement.
– Steve Prefontaine

RUNNING, FOR ME, HAD ALWAYS BEEN A SIMPLE extension of walking, a more efficient way to explore distant pastures and farmlands. Childhood games like tag or football in large part demanded quick running movements. High school track and associated field events included distance running as a core training exercise. Later in life, the military enforced fitness standards by timing mile-and-a-half runs. Running felt natural. It remained that subconscious extension of walking until after I turned thirty-two. Then, it changed.

My new unit, the 774th Tactical Airlift Squadron, resembled any other C-130 aircraft unit with one notable exception. We shared a high level of athleticism. Our Squadron Commander, Lt Col Cliff Hodge, scouted newly assigned officers for athletic ability and quietly moved them to the 774th rather than lose them to either of the other two flying squadrons. His zeal came in part as a tribute to one of our incredibly athletic pilots, Capt Gil Harder, deceased. As Gil neared Annapurna's summit, the world's deadliest 26,200-foot Himalayan peak, an avalanche swept him and two others to their demise.

Not long after this tragic event, I participated in SOLL-II missions. We flew during the darkness of night using early-version night-vision goggles. At the time, I smoked too much and floundered along in disgusting physical shape.

The mission demanded fitness and mental acuity. I knew I could, and should, improve in both categories.

I'd spent a stressful night flying through turbulent air north of El Paso. When I awoke the next morning, the "clue light" came on. I realized that ineffective night vision skyrocketed the inherent risk of flying these missions. Night vision is based on a protein called Rhodopsin which exists in rod cells located at the back of the retina. While a lack of vitamin A reduces the production of Rhodopsin, other things like fatigue, drugs, alcohol, and heavy smoking also reduce one's ability to see at night. I could do better. Decision number one – quit smoking, which I did that morning and haven't smoked since. Decision number two – curb my drinking patterns. Decision number three – start running and set obtainable goals to stay focused.

The early stages of my new running program introduced all the early runner struggles. I struggled to develop a steady breathing pattern and when I did, it soon gave way to boredom. I needed a goal, an internal image of myself gliding through a ten-mile run or just finishing a race.

That's when I noticed the 774th sponsored Gil Harder Biathlon. The fifty-mile cycling course and twenty-six-point-two-mile run could be accomplished either as a team or as an individual. I committed to doing it solo and so began my formal running improvement program.

Three-mile runs wouldn't hack it. I needed to stretch them further and run more often. Every other day, I plodded along gravel farm roads and welcomed detours for their diversity. I ran based on time rather than distance – an hour seemed like a good baseline. On the weekends I'd add a Saturday morning bike ride south to Buffalo Gap and then through undulating oil fields before heading back into Abilene.

I rode a very heavy steel-framed ten-speed bicycle. This beauty seemed cutting-edge years earlier when I bought it in South Korea. A small structural failure forced a change. One of the pedals fell apart thirty miles south of Abilene and only a miracle got me home. I purchased a much lighter replacement bike. Any decent cyclist would consider it an overweight mechanical relic by today's standards. At the time, it represented a huge improvement.

To augment the afternoon running and weekend cycling routine, I joined a local fitness club and swam a mile most mornings before work. Endurance remained sub-world class but my overall fitness improved. The Gil Harder loomed large in my mind. I'd never run any distances close to twenty-six miles during training but convinced myself the need didn't exist. Running became more of a mental game than a physical one. If I developed enough muscle tone and strength to run half a marathon, then mental toughness would carry me through the second half. That seemed like a good plan.

I ran while listening to music for a week before concluding that it hindered me more than it helped. It slowed my pace by nearly fifteen seconds per mile. Maybe boogie-woogie … Instead, I created mental topics before running, things like science trivia, mechanical troubleshooting, or memorizing aircraft limitations. I mentally built aircraft parts and designed instrument panels. Running became a private time to think. I learned to tolerate the Texas heat and savor views of grazing Hereford cattle.

During multi-event races like the Gil Harder Biathlon, transitions became a key component. Cycling tended to contract my calf muscles, and following the transition from cycling to running, my legs felt numb for the first few miles. It amounted to another mental challenge. In training for this eventuality, I often cycled a short twelve-mile loop before running. The numb-leg transition became routine. It helped. During the Gil Harder Biathlon that numb feeling lasted for the first four to five miles.

I quite by accident discovered that eating popcorn before running caused mild stomach cramps. Rather than avoid popcorn, I welcomed the challenge and used it to further toughen my mental state. One side of my brain screamed "STOP!" while the other side resolutely demanded, "Keep moving."

The Gil Harder Biathlon starting gun sounded at 7 a.m. Fingers and toes felt like they'd been dipped in ice water. Frost crystals formed on my bike and windbreaker. Pumping the bike's pedals kept me focused on the road. Twenty-five miles out and twenty-five miles back. It began against a moderate wind. I expended most of my energy before the running even started. The transition happened too quickly.

"Sit and rest before continuing," my body begged, but I couldn't waste the time.

My legs became wooden stumps. They worked but without feeling. I focused on vehicular traffic and then on the runners ahead. I kept running. At ten miles, I began walking, then ran a half-mile and walked the same. Eventually, I caught sight of Meach, another young aircraft commander in our squadron. I gritted my teeth while running until catching him, and we ran together for the remainder of the race. At six miles remaining, he slowed.

"I've got to stop. There's something in my shoe that keeps jabbing me."

He pulled a six-inch nail from the sole of his running shoe and we continued to the finish. It took a little over eight hours. Meach flew an airplane to the east coast early the next morning. I loafed around the house all day, physically spent. My first Gil Harder finish represented success.

I cycled and ran the Gil Harder Biathlon three times with each race being significantly better than the previous one. The Wausau Triathlon in Wisconsin came to my attention as another endurance event during this timeframe.

How hard can it be compared to the Gil Harder?

Wausau ironically existed in Marathon County. The year I participated, the triathlon consisted of a mile-and-a-half lake swim, a twenty-five-mile bike ride, and a 10K run. It seemed relatively benign when I signed up in the flatlands of Texas.

The swim came first with a sequenced start. Swimmers splashed up my back while my head bobbed perilously close to kicking feet ahead of me. Being a strong swimmer helped. I sloshed onshore and found my bike. The transition felt quick, the first five miles of the ride eased by with minimal effort. Then a long, steady hill changed everything. A nearby ski resort boasted a "black route" only slightly more inclined. I think this stretch included part of it. My high spirits deflated, but I kept moving upward and forward. Finally, after losing ground to what seemed like everyone, I dismounted the bike and began running on rubbery legs. I caught many of those who'd whizzed by me earlier on the "hill of death." One last older guy remained within reach. Two miles to go, yet I couldn't close the gap. Despite my best effort, he finished a few seconds ahead of me. I hoped when I reached his age, I'd possess similar strength and endurance. It left a life-long mark.

Flying to exotic destinations held a certain mystique. Key elements of any trip included eating good food, sightseeing, and partying at night. I now added running to that list.

In England, where we deployed for two to three months each year, I ran and cycled throughout East Anglia. A group of us trained for the London Marathon but the scheduling never worked. However, we did enter a half-marathon in Cambridge. The temperatures hovered in the seventies, which felt dreadfully hot for the locals but quite pleasant for those of us from West Texas.

Participants jockeyed for position heading out of Cambridge and proceeding into the surrounding lowland fens. Locals lined the entire course and cheered everyone as they passed. It left me feeling valued regardless of my pace. As the course returned to Cambridge and climbed cobblestone streets toward the finish, I found untapped energy and accelerated past more than a few struggling runners. I clocked an overall pace of 7:20 per mile, my personal best.

We landed in Athens, Greece, for an extended layover, and I couldn't keep myself from running along the coastline before joining the crew for dinner. After an hour of observing pristine beaches and rocky outcroppings, I reversed course. This method of exploring new areas added geographic perspective and cultural immersion. Incredible memories of Athens would never have been possible had I not become an avid runner. This practice repeated itself in England, Italy, Spain, and Turkey as well as most of Asia.

The Marine Corps organized a ten-mile team-oriented run through some local hazards during the time I flew airplanes in the Philippines. The race took place northwest of Manila at Subic Naval Station and required participants to wear uniforms, including fatigues and combat boots. The last team member to finish marked the 4-man-team's finishing time. What a race to remember.

The first half-mile section of entangled bamboo and thorns suited our Air Force approach perfectly. While gung-ho Marines hacked their way through the mess we followed with a chuckle and easy step.

"After all, that's why there're Marines in the first place."

Next, we entered an endless water-filled ditch too deep for walking and too narrow for swimming. Finally, the water ended and I could start running … in soaked combat boots on legs that'd lost all feeling. A mile or two later, the feeling began returning to my legs. The running surface suddenly changed from relatively level to impossibly inclined. I guessed it to be almost forty degrees. Someone ran past me. Unbelievable! He must have been a decoy to demoralize everyone else. More running. The sun beat hotter but then the finish area came into sight.

One last obstacle, a belly crawl through a foot of mud and water, stood between me and the finish line. Overhead barbed wire entrapped us in the muck. One last sprint and I finished. Fun? I'm not so sure even after all these years.

I trained for this event by running five miles during my lunch break or after work. Since the mud run required combat boots, I wore them and eventually learned to run long distances in them. The training course followed a similar diabolical route along a narrow muck-bottomed stream, then up and around a five-hundred-foot hill. It descended back into a rocked-walled canyon with another creek bed. The last segment followed a long incline back toward my neighborhood.

During lunch breaks, I developed a habit of running four to five miles with Freeway, my Brittany Spaniel. Freeway occasionally stressed in the heat and once leaped off a ten-foot bridge into the shallow waters below. He wouldn't come out for fifteen minutes. The runs took my mind off work and I looked forward to them every few days.

Chapter 21

The drinking club with a running problem.
– Selangor Hash House Harrier

THE MOST BEAUTIFUL RUN OF MY LIFE BECAME a possibility one night when my dad stopped by my home in Green Bay, Wisconsin. The topic of the Internet came into our conversation and I explained how a person could search for job postings on a global scale. He found the Internet's global reach more than a bit amazing, so I proposed a random search.

"Name a country you'd like to live in other than the United States."

"New Zealand," he responded.

We found Monster Jobs on the Internet and entered New Zealand. Sure enough, a hotel management job listing for Lake Tekapo appeared. My mom and dad had spent a memorable night at that very location.

Later while sitting alone at the computer, I emailed the hotel owner with a series of questions. After numerous exchanges, we agreed to split expenses for a visit the following week. My immersion into Kiwi culture started when he met me at Christchurch airport. His goal included convincing me to manage his operation, and I wanted to know more about New Zealand. The area stole my breath with its beauty. No billboards or gaudy buildings spoiled the scenic mountainsides. Pristine lakes sparkled with turquoise-colored water. The air tasted fresh and cool under clear blue skies.

Early on my first morning, I donned running gear and jogged upward along a pine-tree pathway toward the University of Canterbury's Mt. John Observatory. Every corner of New Zealand appeared incredibly gorgeous. I'd never felt so free and unencumbered.

My heart and soul embraced Tekapo's tiny community and told me to stay. Unfortunately, the business faced significant competition, declining cash flow, and major staffing challenges. The only school consisted of one large room that accommodated students from kindergarten through high school, and I only noticed a handful in total. I ultimately wrote a detailed business plan and declined his offer. But I never forgot the most beautiful run of my life. Ironically, one of the most interesting weeks of my life remained unknown to all but my wife. I didn't think others would find it interesting, until now.

Quite by accident, I came into contact with a group called the Hash House Harriers. This international organization focused on having fun while running. I hadn't realized their origins went back to a time when several British colonial officers and expatriates formed the group in late 1938 in Selangor, Malaysia.

After World War Two, Kuala Lumpur hashers received word from the Registrar of Societies that, since they comprised a "group," they required a constitution. Four Hash House Harriers, or HHH, objectives subsequently came to life, as recorded on the 1950 club registration card:

- To promote physical fitness among our members
- To get rid of weekend hangovers
- To acquire a good thirst and to satisfy it in beer
- To persuade the older members that they are not as old as they feel

The organization grew. There are currently almost two thousand chapters throughout the world, including two operating in Antarctica.

During a hash run, one or more members called "hares" lay a trail, which is then followed by the remainder of the group called the "pack." Sawdust, flour, powdered milk, shredded paper, or chalk, are routinely used to mark the trail. The trail periodically ends at a "check" and the pack must find where it begins again. Often the trail includes false starts, shortcuts, dead ends, back-checks, and splits. These features are designed to keep the pack together despite differences in fitness level or running speed, as front-runners are forced to slow down to find the "true" trail, allowing stragglers to catch up.

I began running with the Angeles City HHH while stationed in the Philippines and ran hashes with San Fernando, Subic Bay, Puerto Galera, and several in Manila. I also ran hashes in Korea, Okinawa, mainland Japan, Thailand, Guam, the lower United States, and Hawaii.

The runs averaged four to six miles but I've spent hours running through sweltering-hot sugarcane fields as far as ten miles. Most often, they transited areas a normal person would never frequent, from the worst city slums to remote jungles to inland rivers and ocean shores.

One sticky-hot Friday night in Bangkok, with pungent street smells filling motionless air, I found myself in the dimly lit New Orleans Bar and Restaurant. Our commander, Col Lee "Papasan" Hess, raved about their red beans and rice. The scotch met his quality standards and the staff engaged in fun-loving banter. When I inquired about hashing, an Indian hotel manager joined the conversation and mentioned that he'd be running the Bangkok Hash scheduled the next morning. Several of us agreed to meet him and ride along to the event.

At 9 a.m. I stood alone in the tiny lobby of his hotel. The rest slept in and missed an experience of a lifetime. We climbed into his rusted-out VW Beetle and chugged along toward the countryside. To my great relief, he stopped along a grassy area in front of a large Buddhist temple an hour later. It felt irreverent parking so close, but what did I know? Others arrived. We walked toward an open river behind the temples.

Two 50-foot-long dragon boats bobbed in the water along a makeshift wooden dock. These sleek vessels had ornately carved dragon heads at the bow and dragon tails aft. We found seating on wooden slats, an inch of water sloshing against our feet, and eased into the Chao Phraya River current. Little by little the jungle closed in until we glided under a canopy of overhanging jungle growth.

"There! Stop at that concrete pad."

It consisted of an eight-foot square along the river bank. Someone spotted shredded paper and the hash began.

The jungle swallowed us after the first few steps. The damp freshness of trees and bushes filled our lungs. We traversed creeks and drainage ditches via crude bamboo bridges consisting of one or two poles laid across the water. Structures and people existed elsewhere, yet the hint of smoke in the air betrayed their presence. The trail disappeared on and off for the next two hours. After a seemingly endless chase, we discovered another eight-foot concrete pad jutting into another jungle-encroached river. A blue Igloo cooler occupied the far corner. We'd found the finish point.

Within minutes, the jungle darkened and night settled upon us. I wondered how I'd have followed a minimally marked trail in the darkness of the jungle. The thought prompted me to drink another beer.

We drank and shared crazy recollections of the chase. Another adventure. Everyone lived in the moment … our normal world existed somewhere else. Then two dragon boats appeared from the shadows. We climbed on board and disappeared back into the darkness of the river. I loved hashing.

Okinawa's hash opened my eyes to the mountainous nature of the island. I'd only run around Kadena Air Base, which seemed relatively flat. Then I connected with the local hash and ran elsewhere on the island where none of the hash trails remotely resembled flat. Night runs along sandy beaches and through bushy hillsides miraculously avoided poisonous habu snakes and other deadly critters. We lost ourselves in late-night bar districts, in traditional villages, and along deserted beaches. The experiences felt … well … unusual.

The more avid Okinawa HHH runners got excited about the Naha Marathon. Our starting positions would be determined on individual per-mile-paces. My starting position fell well back into the overall mass of runners, too far back. It took almost four minutes before I passed the official start point after the starting gun fired.

My goals for this marathon included finishing in under four hours. Running a slow eight-minute pace would get me to the finish line in just under three and a half. It seemed reasonable at the time. The first portion of the course weaved through downtown Naha, then began a slow uphill climb. I felt fresh and ran well ahead of my programmed pace. The last half of the course consisted of a long downhill portion followed by a relatively flat eight-mile stretch to the finish line.

The downhill stretch proved my Waterloo as cartilage wrapping the sides of my knees became inflamed with the added pounding of the slope. Japanese bystanders offered some sort of pain-killing spray which I welcomed for the next several miles. But I knew if I kept using it, I'd likely suffer longer-lasting cartilage damage. I walked, ran, walked some more, and struggled. Somewhere around the five-hour mark, I crossed the finish line. The lesson learned proved valuable. Push, but don't get carried away. It applied to more than just running.

Chapter 22

I don't run to add days to my life, I run to add life to my days.
– Ronald Rook

YEARS LATER, AS A CONTRACTOR IN TOKYO, I'd lost contact with the Hash House Harriers. The active hashers existed much farther into the metropolitan area and I didn't look forward to an hour-long train ride to get to and from events. But I came to know a local running group called the Yokota Striders. They focused on traditional running, and they had the resources to participate in marathons throughout the region.

In Japan, a marathon didn't necessarily equate to a twenty-six-point-two-mile race, but rather a running event in general. Most marathons featured a 5km, a 10km, a 20km, and occasionally a 40km race. I found it refreshing to run with the Japanese, who represented the most running-obsessed culture I'd ever experienced. Their second-largest televised sporting event remains a two-day "ekiden" relay race. Many large corporations sponsor employee teams to participate in the event.

The Chiba Suica Marathon, or watermelon run, the Yokohama Marathon, the Kanagawa "Grape" Marathon, and others attracted runners of all sizes. Eight-year-old children ran alongside eighty-year-old seniors. Our group included a seventy-year-old woman who ventured into running only a few years earlier. Others wore colorful costumes or stylish shirts, shorts, and tights. Running with the Striders became festive and fun. It expanded my view of the athletic and fun-loving Japanese people.

Seventy percent of Japan is mountainous with thousands of trails crisscrossing the country. Eric Fitzpatrick, the President of the Strider's Running Club, told me that mountain trails capped every accessible ridge. We naturally searched for ways to get from the valleys to those ridges and once there we ran along isolated pathways. Eric possessed incredible strength and endurance. Where he glided across trails, I struggled. He throttled back while I pushed to keep up. We stayed within sight of each other while expanding our world.

Japanese locals believe the gods live in the mountains, and many of the trails came into existence to assist spiritual trekkers in their ascent to the peak. Invariably they'd find a shrine dedicated to the gods, many of which exist to this day.

Mountain running proved to be a grueling experience. But in return, the trails offered expansive panoramas, cloud-buffered solitude, and cool fresh air. Eric and I quickly became hooked.

The Armed Forces News network featured our trail running in one of their human-interest spots and for a week we became noteworthy. During the summer months, we scooted home from work and undertook a short trail run before sunset. On weekends, we departed early in the morning in search of new trailheads. We ran for hours before dragging ourselves back home.

Each year in October, Eric's wife and I supported him during a Japanese mountain endurance race called the Tsuneo Hasegawa Cup. This relatively new race first appeared in 1992. The year prior, a respected Japanese mountaineer by the same name died at the age of forty-three in an avalanche while attempting to climb Ultar Two in

Pakistan's Karakoram Mountain Range. He trained for his mountaineering expeditions in the local mountains surrounding Okutama, and Tokyo businessmen sponsored this annual event in his memory.

Hasegawa is not a run for the faint-hearted as it spans forty-four-point-five miles with a cumulative elevation gain of fifteen thousand feet. The starting gun fires relatively late in the day at 1 p.m. which forces competitors to endure a long and challenging overnight run. Eric finished around 3 a.m.

My role included driving high into the mountains, parking at a remote mining museum, and then finding the pathway leading much higher into the mountains. Where the path intercepted the race trail, we waited for Eric so we could supply him with Granola Bars and water. This violated the rule prohibiting in-race support.

By the time I parked the car, darkness, cold, and relentless drizzle dominated the mountains. The thirty-minute hike up the steep and winding path required flashlights. We eventually intercepted the Hasegawa trail and knew it to be the right spot because an emergency support team had set up their treatment tent in the saddle between two blackened mountain peaks. There seemed no way to determine the slope of the ridge until the runners began appearing out of the sky.

All wore headlamps and appeared as specks of light high above. At first, I thought I saw a shooting star, but then it reversed course across the sky. When it continued coming closer, I realized that I'd been watching a runner's headlamp. Soon, the next two shooting stars zig-zagged toward us … and then a few more. Eventually, Eric appeared, tired, supported on mud-caked legs and shoes. He beamed a smile knowing we'd smuggled additional water and energy bars. The rules struck me as being overly brutal. Over the years participants died running this race.

When Eric gathered enough energy to continue, he disappeared up an equally steep, muddy slope.

Running set me on a better course for life. I became fit and resolute in meeting challenges. But more importantly, I came to terms with my body and my mental outlook. Running provided isolation from the stresses of the world, it turned my thoughts inward and focused on positive things. I noticed nature's beauty. I designed aircraft parts. I developed stories for future books. Running became extremely therapeutic.

Chapter 23

There are no great limits to growth because there are no limits of human intelligence, imagination, and wonder.
– Ronald Reagan

THERE COMES A TIME FOR EVERY YOUNG AIR Force pilot when he takes the first step away from the cockpit. For most, it represents a positive career move, something anticipated and expected. For a few, it becomes a foot-dragging, "Please, I don't wanna go" experience. Any guesses as to how I felt?

Our new squadron commander, Lt Col Charles Fortenberry, called me into his office.

"I've got a great opportunity for you."

A lot of not-so-good opportunities start with that phrase. I instantly became all ears. And anxious.

"There's an opening in the Command Post and the DO wants to improve the controller-aircrew interface. You're the perfect person for the job. Are you interested?"

Command Post. No one wants to get stuck there.

"As an aircrew scheduler, my experience might contribute even more working Current Operations. Is there any chance of that?"

"Right now, your only option is Command Post," he replied.

I smiled knowing it'd be all or nothing.

"When can I start? Thanks for believing in me."

Never in my wildest dreams could I have imagined the bizarre twists that awaited me.

Learning the aircraft controller position didn't seem the least bit complicated. I'd reference and update several floor-to-ceiling back-lit grease boards that dominated the front wall. Each night I'd meticulously transcribe the daily flying schedule onto the left panel. The right panel displayed the status of all off-station aircraft and I'd update it as changes took place. It occurred to me that while the process took quite a bit of time to post, it didn't capture a historical record of daily events and it didn't allow for data sharing. Grease boards had been around forever. It'd be tough dreaming up a viable alternative.

The messaging part of the job seemed a bit more complex and often involved classified materials and equipment. It allowed for rapid communication of important things, like going to war and reporting mission-impacting damage after tornadoes, or aircraft accidents.

The most enjoyable challenge involved talking to the aircrew over the UHF radio. They universally hated calling Command Post controllers because delayed responses made the calls seem unnecessary. I found it much more interesting to anticipate what crewmembers would ask and then answer their questions before they asked.

I thoroughly enjoyed putting a young co-pilot or navigator behind the mental power curve while at the same time letting him experience my version of excellence. I loved it. Others thought it weird.

Working twelve-hour shifts allowed for an extra day off each week. I committed a lot of time to building an experimental Q-2 foam and fiberglass aircraft and the extra day helped. This Command Post job seemed perfect.

One night, I walked into the control room.

"Where's TSgt Smith? He should be here on shift."
"He's in the Crisis Action Team room."

The terse response seemed strange.

I found him stretched out and sound asleep atop the massive conference table that dominated the room.

"Get up! Go home! You're NOT working tonight."

He entered alcohol rehab the next day and I found out that I'd handled his situation all wrong. I didn't know any better but probably should have. Fortunately for TSgt Smith, he never submitted to a blood-alcohol test or been officially declared drunk while on duty. Either of those situations would likely have led to his separation from the Air Force. I watched him more closely and talked with him often over the following months.

He went on to serve quite successfully in Japan, became a Master Sergeant, and most importantly, managed his personal life far more effectively. One career saved.

On the night of March 12, 1985, I responded to a telephone call notifying me that one of our C-130s had crashed moments earlier at Fort Hood. The aircraft became too slow, stalled over the drop zone, and pancaked onto the ground while attempting to drop three containerized delivery bundles. Six of eight crewmembers on the aircraft perished in the fiery aftermath.

Over the next eighteen hours, I juggled many phone calls, wrote FLASH reports to the Pentagon, and talked with the Texas State Police, our Wing Commander, and many, many others.

Eventually, I passed the phones to a replacement and dragged myself home, exhausted. The day pulled emotions in all directions, a stressful, sad, yet strangely exhilarating night.

I'd lost interest in solving the grease board inefficiencies when an unexpected modernization option encroached upon the status quo.

Several Zenith Z100 computers arrived and we placed three of them in our control room. We had little understanding of software programs or what they did. The Internet seemed more a pipedream than a reality, and the word "e-mail" had barely entered the English lexicon. Think of a barely recognizable trail in the jungle and then think of an eight-lane interstate highway. That describes the difference between the internet then and the internet now.

The Air Force's first major desktop computer, the Zenith Z100.

A young and computer-savvy Staff Sergeant knew of a mobility program written by several young officers at Altus Air Force Base. One unique aspect of their program involved a dual-monitor display. This technology didn't exist yet. Color displays required three memory chips, one for each primary color, but our new Air Force computers included only the green color chip. We bought additional chips from a parts house in California and then burrowed into the console, under the keyboard, and inserted an additional chip into the blue slot.

The Altus programmers used MS-DOS to write their program and had "poked" memory locations for the green and blue color chips. This "poking" data routed it to either one color or the other. By splitting the video cable, we could add a second monitor and display a separate screen of data, one screen for green data and the other for blue data.

My "idea" light came on.

By borrowing the mobility program's "poke" coding, I created a Local Training green screen display and a second, Off-Station Mission blue screen display.

MS-DOS allowed users to navigate, open, and otherwise manipulate files from a command line at the bottom of the screen. Only after entering the data and hitting the Enter Key did the information write to memory. It felt awkward and not entirely intuitive, but it represented a starting point. Graphical User Interfaces, or GUIs, are today's standard for data input but they didn't exist at the time. We became creative and had fun in our private, geeky world.

My basic controller job challenged me in a variety of ways. I loved the positive feeling inherent in programming. Remaining one step ahead of the aircrews who called for "easy to anticipate" information provided additional pleasure. Two of us made promotions to Major and when our Command Post Chief got orders directing his imminent departure, the Director of Operations selected me as his logical replacement. What! My comfortable world suddenly turned upside down with leadership responsibilities I never anticipated. On the other hand, it provided another step in the right direction.

"I'm honored that you've considered me for this challenging position. We've got a lot of irons in the fire and I promise to manage each of them to the best of my ability. Thank you."

Col Hanson Scott, the new Wing Commander, settled into his routine. He appeared in the command post unusually early one morning.

"Tell me about the computer program," he asked one of the controllers

"It's great," she replied, "but it takes almost two hours to update everything, and then we have to do the grease boards as well."

Later that day, the commander pulled me aside.

"You need to reduce the time to input the computer data. Once that's done, we can think about eliminating the grease boards."

Hours upon hours of coding in GW-Basic followed. I wrote a lengthy subroutine to highlight individual data fields. It allowed for updates to be entered in the exact spot on the screen where it appeared, not at the bottom of the screen. It streamlined data entry significantly. Input time dropped from hours to twenty minutes. Data entered meant data saved. The archived file captured a daily record of everything.

The bigger time-saver, however, happened when I wrote a new sub-routine that copied the current day's off-station missions to the next day's file. It eliminated another hour of needless key punching!

Over time, we bundled the flight-following program with weather depictions and daily briefing slides and then piped it all to the Wing Commander's and the Director of Operations' office computers. They simply rotated a selector knob to view whatever interested them. They loved it.

Goodbye grease boards!

The Command Post staff had always been limited, with only a handful of officers and a few enlisted controllers. It soon shrunk in the worst possible way.

Chapter 24

Millions saw the apple fall, but Newton was the one who asked why.
– Benard Baruch

ONE OF OUR YOUNG AIRMEN HAD RECENTLY moved off base to share an apartment with a friend. That friendship turned sour during a late-night argument. Following a blow to the back of the head with a lead pipe, our airman fell unconscious. A ventilator sustained his "brain-dead" body for another week. Distraught parents flew from Tiffin, Ohio, and eventually made arrangements to have his deceased body returned home.

I felt their grief each day. Coordinating with mortuary affairs, commanders, the family, and the office filled every minute of every day. A week later I accompanied the casket to Tiffin, interfaced with the funeral home manager, and arranged to have an Honor Guard support his memorial service. I felt emotionally drained.

Three weeks later, our Non-Commissioned Officer In Charge ran his annual aerobics test at the base track. Shortly thereafter, I received a phone call advising me that an ambulance had transported him to the hospital. An undiagnosed heart issue caused his heart to seize. He died within seconds of clutching his chest.

A Technical Sergeant controller, who'd been his best friend, dealt with mortuary affairs. Unbelievable. We operated in a subdued environment for weeks

Two months later, one of the officers developed some sort of medical issue that caused him to miss nearly a month of work. The Director of Operations called me to his office and explained the situation.

Doctors diagnosed the young captain with clinical depression and prescribed lead-based pills. This treatment caused his security clearance to be suspended and that disqualified him from performing controller duties.

"Can you keep him busy each day while keeping him out of the control room?" the commander asked.

"I think I have just the answer. Let's see how it goes."

In the weeks that followed I taught him to program using GW-Basic coding. Learning to code wouldn't be difficult but learning the flight-following program with all its subroutines did present a challenge.

Each morning, I assigned him several focus areas along with program elements I wanted changed. I then reviewed his previous day's coding, made suggestions where necessary, and moved forward. This arrangement did little to satisfy our short-handed staffing issues, but it did keep the young Captain productive until he recovered. A second career saved.

One additional project that remained in the background concerned the complete renovation of the entire command post. My predecessor managed the design reviews and temporary facility arrangements. We awaited military construction funding, and of course, approval came amidst all the other turmoil affecting our operations.

We spent a weekend moving all the desks, cabinets, and computers into several bare-bones mobile homes.

"Damn, what a mess."

The Director of Operations called me to his office.

"I've got a possible assignment for you. It's in the Communications Directorate at Military Airlift Command. If you're interested I'll have you nominated for the position."

This sounded great. I knew a staff job probably existed somewhere for me. In all likelihood, it wouldn't include flying, but moving seemed inevitable.

Comm, that's the last place I want to get stuck. There'll be no wiggle room on this one. Take it or ... or ... I guess I need to take it.

"You'll be working on a classified program," he continued. "I don't know many details but it's considered a high priority. You'll be managing the Special Operations Command and Control Upgrade Program."

During my time at the Command Post, I'd built an experimental aircraft. The project materialized when another more technical pilot and good friend, Bob Grieder, drew my attention to a plane called the Q-2. The odd-looking aircraft took shape by carving foam and covering it with various layers of fiberglass. Side-by-side seating appealed to me and its top-end airspeed of one hundred and sixty knots could reach far-away destinations rather quickly. After ordering the plans and building materials, I built a large workbench in the garage, and waited ...

On the day the shipment arrived, I took inventory and stacked everything in the garage. The only components that looked like airplane parts appeared to be the wheels and tires. The rest consisted of foam blocks, long rolls of fiberglass cloth, tubes, nuts, and bolts.

Did I just throw away seven thousand dollars?

Eighteen-hour days in the garage became the norm when not working shifts or running. A year passed ...

Bob and his wife Ginny came by and spent a day helping fiberglass the wings.

Quickie Q-2 Experimental Aircraft - N774TM

Eventually, it looked complete. I leased a hangar at Abilene Muni and proceeded to engine runs and taxi tests. Life got interesting ...

The cheap radio I'd purchased struggled to transmit. After reworking the electrical ground plane, I finally got it working but only when it wanted to work. It represented the first of several issues I'd need to overcome.

Between thirty and fifty knots, the tail wheel lost effectiveness because it'd been designed too small. The rudder didn't become effective until fifty, so a short window of "no directional control" existed. It didn't cause any problems until I planned ground runs at forty knots before knowing of the controllability issue. After almost clipping a taxiway light, I wrote to Quickie Corporation. They responded that they'd recently discovered the issue.

The first attempted runway flight prompted split-second decision-making. Everything through the lift-off happened exactly as anticipated. Then the plane banked slightly left toward an American Airlines hangar. Two choices and no time – add power, climb over the hangar, and then continue the left turn to line up on the runway for a landing. Or I could chop power, land in the grass, and swallow my pride.

Option one screamed, "Don't do it!" Into the grass I went and entered a wet area. The tail came up, and the prop buried itself in the mud. A splash of water convinced me the fuel header tank had ruptured and I'd been doused with fuel.

I opened the canopy and jumped out, looking for a fire that would surely engulf me. But I felt dry. It'd been water and not fuel that splashed. I didn't consider this to be an official crash, but simply a bad day. A guy from American Airlines helped me pull the plane back to my hangar.

I found and fixed the cause of the right turn and repaired all the damage. At least, I thought I'd gotten everything.

One of the wheel bearings had become wet and later, during a high-speed taxi test, failed. The bearing seized on the aluminum axle and spun it as I tried to taxi clear of the runway. An American Airlines commuter flight would arrive in twenty minutes and I sat stuck on the high-speed runway exit. In other words, I needed to move the airplane, quickly. The Tower Controller sent a maintenance man in a pickup truck to drag my troublesome aircraft off the runway. Together, he and I lifted the frozen wheel onto an undercar creeper. We once again pulled the plane back to my hangar. That summarizes my last aircraft taxi attempt at Abilene Muni and I'm certain the airport staff felt relieved when I loaded the plane on a trailer and moved it to Illinois.

Chapter 25

Whether you think you can, or you think you can't, you're probably right.
– Henry Ford

I TRAILERED THE EXPERIMENTAL AIRCRAFT behind an old Chevy Caprice to Scott AFB, Illinois. The darned thing pulled well at highway speeds and much to my surprise didn't try to fly toward the side of the interstate. I liked Illinois right away. It didn't feel exactly like Wisconsin, but it reminded me a lot of Wisconsin. Belleville and O'Fallon felt like country towns where much of the base population resided. I rented a small house in Belleville and went looking for my office.

The new staff position spanned two major commands: Military Airlift Command and Air Force Communications Command. The work fell mostly under the first, and that proved to be a good thing. Military Airlift Command, or MAC, controlled aircraft. It represented my link to future flying.

I hoped for an office in the main headquarters building, but the building numbers didn't match. I eventually found the building number painted on an old and isolated wooden structure hidden on the far side of the flight line. Finding a parking place didn't pose the problem like at the main headquarters and that felt good. But I also felt disappointed finding myself out of mainstream staff work. Disappointment faded quickly. I'd landed in a great organization.

The failed 1980 Iranian hostage rescue attempt that left charred aircraft at Desert One prompted an in-depth review of special operations capabilities. Congress vowed to resolve those issues and the Special Operations Forces Command and Control Upgrade Program resulted. I'd replace a young Lieutenant Colonel who recently departed to command McGuire Air Force Base's Communications Squadron.

Right out of the gate, I looked for associated program documents and found scant few. From what I gathered, a generalized list of communications equipment had been funded to the tune of twelve-point-four million dollars. Once I completed the purchases, I'd conclude the program. To me, this looked more like a splash of money rather than a program. I sensed the upgrade program would be incomplete, poorly planned, and temporary. It needed a further vision and at least several more years of funding to reach it.

How could I change such a thing?

During the following weeks, I reached out to MAC's special operations office. They knew nothing of my program and pointed me toward 23rd Air Force. At the time, 23rd Air Force managed the rescue and recovery mission. However, it'd soon deactivate with the creation of Air Force Special Operations Command. Colonel Frank Purdy, the Hurlburt AFB Communications Commander became my key operational contact for technical requirements. He'd been a communications specialist by background, understood the need for a more comprehensive approach, and he got results. His primary action officer, Captain Mike

DeHart, worked tirelessly to find the best equipment to satisfy current and projected needs. DeHart and I became great friends and spent much of our time analyzing and sourcing the optimal equipment choices.

The Intelligence side of the program required many of the same computers and communications equipment. A crusty old Lieutenant Colonel named Joe "Two Dogs" Murphy at 23rd Air Force became my contact. Before actually meeting Two Dogs, I considered him to be opinionated and forceful. I harbored no doubt he'd be a difficult partner. Then we met and all that changed. He provided great insight and justification for his requirements. Over the years, he'd become legendary within the world of special operations. His old-school, rough-around-the-edges approach added a great deal of charisma to his rock-solid knowledge.

Core staff during the creation of AFSOC Communications. (Seated) Col Frank Purdy (L-R) Capt Mike Hudgens, Maj Scott Ellis, Lt Col Howard Benton, Maj Mike DeHart, and Maj Terry Mallon.

The most critical cog in the wheel, Lieutenant Colonel Howard Benton, resided at the Pentagon. He helped quantify the requirements and coordinated funding justifications, and more importantly, sources. Benton served as the Program Element Manager, the man who got the money.

I needed to get my hands around the program, to understand its intent and scope, what needed to be purchased, and over what time frame. A single program document contained bits and pieces of these elements but seemed too vague to properly define a path forward.

I authored two documents that better defined the program. A SOFC2 Architecture document identified overall shortfalls, provided Congressional direction on building capability, and laid out a multi-year course of action. I assigned notional funding targets. The second document addressed specific equipment needs, manning allocations, and facility shortfalls. It detailed both near-term and longer-term solutions.

Once coordinated and approved, these two documents justified my existence on the staff. I knew what had to be done and worked long hours learning how to buy things. Four key areas took shape.

DeHart and I traveled around the country attending tradeshows and vendor exhibitions. We worked with Army Special Forces and Navy Seals to determine interoperable radios and computer systems. In the end, we developed a comprehensive equipment list. I worked with joint-service acquisition offices to squeeze our requisitions into existing contracts whenever possible.

A second acquisition area presented much greater challenges. To deploy tactical mission planning cells, we planned to purchase bread-truck-type vehicles. A total of six, three for operations and three for intelligence would be manufactured. They'd be deployed either by driving them to a forward operating location or by airlifting them in the back of a C-130. They carried extra fuel and ran special generators integrated into the frame.

The simple panel van that I first envisioned wouldn't work because the equipment weighed too much. It required additional framing, making the vans really expensive. I didn't feel good about this solution but the special operators felt otherwise. I wondered if a better solution existed, an out-of-the-box answer to the core issue of moving equipment to a forward operating location. I couldn't think of one and we pushed forward with the vans. The government eventually signed the custom vehicle contract and the manufacturing process began … and lasted six months before the company filed for bankruptcy.

"Nessie," the Naval Electronic Systems Engineering Activity in Saint Inigoes, Maryland managed several classified projects. Lt Col Benton had contacts and somehow got them to take over the vehicle integration. In a nutshell, they got the vans released from Chapter 11 proceedings, visited the manufacturer's site, seized anything related to their construction, and moved the project to Saint Inigoes.

It became a stressful process, but Nessie eventually delivered all six vans to Hurlburt Field, Florida. They appeared clunky, underpowered, and barely able to fit in the back of a C-130. But they existed and brought a new and unique capability to the Air Force.

The third acquisition area concerned personnel. All of this equipment required operators and maintainers. We'd create three new communications squadrons. The authority for all of this resided in my approved program documents. That summarized the extent of my contribution. Col Purdy developed a manpower list of specialties. Lt Col Benton scrounged the Air Force for rescinded manpower billets and moved unused positions across the Air Force to our program. Ultimately, twenty-man special operations communications elements came into existence at Clark Air Base in the Philippines, Rhein-Main Air Base in Germany, and Hurlburt Fld in Florida.

The final acquisition area concerned new facilities at each of the above locations. If we kept each project's construction cost below two-hundred-and-fifty-thousand dollars, they'd be considered minor construction. This tactic avoided the time-consuming and competitive process required for major construction projects.

Tradeshows, equipment presentations, construction reviews, program briefings for the receiving units, Congressional hearings, and Pentagon presentations consumed my limited time. It became a precious commodity. I didn't miss flying nearly as much as I anticipated, and found myself preoccupied with developing units and facilities ... and buying things.

Chapter 26

Great leaders are almost always great simplifiers who can cut through argument, debate, and doubt to offer a solution everybody can understand.
– Gen Colin Powell

THE Q-2 AIRCRAFT NEEDED A HOME. IT ALSO needed another first flight. Sparta's Hunter Field, forty miles south of Belleville, offered the perfect solution, and I leased a small hangar. It felt like a sleepy airfield that hosted a sky-diving club with a very friendly staff. Its asphalt runway stretched seventy-five feet across and four thousand feet long, more than enough for test flights.

I'd completed all preparations. Taxi tests passed. The time for a planned flight neared. I planned to fly a single closed pattern, land, analyze everything, and then do it all again. The forty-knot controllability issue flashed through my mind.

Please don't turn left or right once airborne. Don't nose up and stall. I could be dead in a heap within the next sixty seconds. It's time to go.

I test-flew many aircraft before, but after having ground-tested this one, I approached flying with a different mindset. All the construction, the airfoils, the weight and balance, everything, had been my responsibility. I pushed the throttle to maximum power. Take-off, the turn to crosswind, then downwind, and lever-off proceeded perfectly. I decided to fly the airplane at a slightly higher approach speed until reaching the runway threshold. I focused on decelerating airspeed and smooth control response.

I planned to reduce the throttle to idle and endure an extended flare until touchdown. As I flared, the runway suddenly disappeared when the nose came up. The front canard blocked my side view of the surface below. Fingers crossed. Touchdown. The plane flew as predicted, and the feeling of accomplishment surged.

Several months later, I flew the Q-2 to Scott Air Force Base's 4th of July Airshow. Naturally, the radio failed and the tower had to approve my landing via a light signal. The return flight to Sparta marked the last time I flew the Q-2.

The satisfaction of building the aircraft easily outweighed that of flying it. It took eighteen months of long days and nights, hangar costs, and several long-distance moves to get it fully certified. And, I didn't kill myself in the process. I proved to myself that I could do just about anything if I set goals, exerted effort, and stuck with them until fruition. Obtaining Eagle Scout rank, graduating from college, flight school, and my master's degree all required the same intangible elements.

Promotion played a far bigger role in the minds of others than it did in mine. It seemed to me that accomplishing promotion prerequisites over which I had control would be a good start. That's why, as soon as I became eligible, I enrolled in a master's degree program and finished Squadron Officer's School, Air Command and Staff College, and Air War College. Another major contributor to getting promoted focused on job performance. My mantra had been to a*lways do my best and take what I get.*

Word came that I'd been promoted to Lieutenant Colonel. Reassignment orders would follow shortly.

The Director of the Military Airlift Command Communications Directorate called me to his office.

"Terry, I can offer you a Squadron Commander position at one of our wings. It'll take you out of flying. I can't help you there."

I thanked him for his faith in my ability but explained that at my core, I loved flying too much. I wanted to fly regardless of the command potential.

I'd have to move quickly. Capt Mark Volchef sat at the officer assignments desk in the headquarters building. I introduced myself and proceeded to make my case.

"I'd like to be considered for assignment to Clark Air Base in the Philippines, to the 1st Special Operations Squadron. Here's why I think it makes sense. My background is now a mix of conventional C-130 time, Special Operations Low-Level time, and Special Operations staff time. But an even better reason is to save you a lot of heartburn. I know that for every officer you tag to fill a slot in the Philippines, a fair number will opt out of the Air Force. If they do go, they'll be unhappy. I, on the other hand, want to go and I'll be happy for the opportunity. Everyone wins."

He asked me to check back in a week or two.

The last Wing Commander I supported when running the Dyess Command Post, now Brigadier General Hansen Scott, became the Vice Commander of the newly formed Air Force Special Operations Command. I contacted him asking for career advice and the possibility of staying in the world of special operations. He suggested I seek an assignment in AC-130 gunships. It'd been his background and his bias surfaced.

In the end, an assignment to MC-130Es at Clark Air Base came my way. I envisioned myself as a line pilot flying challenging missions in a super-capable aircraft. I'd be a pilot again. What could be better?

Chapter 27

You start with a bag full of luck and an empty bag of experience. The trick is to fill the bag of experience before you empty the bag of luck.
– Unknown.

Hurlburt Field held memories of recent visits associated with the Special Operations Forces Command and Control Upgrade Program. This time I'd begin the tedious process of learning the complex, highly capable MC-130E systems and flight procedures. Flying at 250 feet above the ground in mountainous terrain with stormy skies could be intimidating, but for me, it proved just the opposite. Know the systems. Trust the displays. Anticipate. Anticipate, Anticipate. Challenge accepted.

We pushed through low-hanging clouds along Florida's panhandle heading north under and around late-night thunderstorms. The Appalachian Mountains heightened the challenge, rewarding success with an addictive rush of accomplishment. Flying low in the inky darkness of mountain valleys with only a radar presentation to guide the aircraft around them kept me on the razor's edge. Once we landed, that sense of success remained only until the next flight when the slate wiped itself clean and the challenge presented itself all over again.

Two written exams and a flight check. I boarded a C-141 cargo plane headed for the Philippines.

Lt Col Terry Sylvester, the 1st Special Operations Squadron Commander, and one of the most respected officers I've known, greeted me at the unit. I became an Assistant Director of Operations until they could find something better for me to do.

What happened to being a regular pilot and learning the mission? I'd be expected to know which end is up and I'd have very limited experience on which to base judgments.

Before my household goods arrived, and more importantly, before I received warm clothes, I departed for Alaska on some sort of exercise. Anchorage in October felt pretty darned cold, and my wardrobe consisted of a threadbare flight suit and a few polo shirts.

The flight droned on for an incredible fifteen hours and included three aerial refuelings. I walked around the cargo compartment a lot to stay warm. I'd be a passenger on this flight. That is until I visited the cockpit and took the co-pilot's seat while he disappeared into the cargo compartment. Six and a half hours later, he returned for our second refueling.

Shortly after landing and minutes before freezing to death, I purchased the warmest wool-knit sweater I've ever owned. It warmed me during the next several weeks and took up space in a drawer for years thereafter.

We flew an orientation flight on the first day. Alaska's natural beauty and majestic expanses must have been a glimpse of heaven. Glaciers looked like frozen lava, frosty mountaintops reached toward the sky, and raging rivers cut deep into valley floors. Then we entered the clouds and flew in terrain-following mode.

We crested ridges at 175 feet and then pushed the nose down and descended along the far slope of the terrain. Doing this while in the clouds felt … well, interesting. Imagine flying inside a ping pong ball surrounded by an unfocused light-gray mist. Only 250 feet below us, a tumbling river wove its way from higher terrain. To either side, sheer, snow-covered slopes disappeared into grayish clouds. We climbed higher into the "grayness" knowing it masked craggy rocks. A ridge passed below us. We stared at huge, jagged boulders within arm's reach. At that moment, I pushed the yoke forward and descended back into the unfocused white.

Please don't crash! Please don't crash!

We continued toward the next ridge. It felt like playing a game except it embraced reality. Loss of concentration invited disaster. We survived, and I loved it.

There'd only be one daytime orientation flight. We shifted to middle-of-the-night missions where we fought freezing temperatures and moderate turbulence before airdropping personnel and supplies into remote mountainous locations.

Back in Anchorage, fish sandwiches and baked salmon fillets surpassed anything I'd experienced before, including Wisconsin's Friday night perch fries. I found myself flying again, and the 1st Special Operations Squadron elevated the experience to an incredible new level.

Flying in central Luzon offered its share of interesting flights as well. One day we departed Clark Air Base on a visual flight plan and found ourselves under a low overcast before entering the Sierra Madre Mountains north of Manila.

The farther we flew, the lower the clouds dipped. The turbulence that first shook us as "mild chop" worsened to moderate jolts, rattling the aircraft and blurring the instruments. We flew into the clouds and controlled the aircraft with absolute reference to those blurred instruments. Intercom chatter lessened to near silence.

We flew below Manila Approach Control's arriving and departing commercial airliners who crossed several thousand feet above us. We couldn't climb. We also didn't want to get violated for flying in the clouds on a visual flight plan. Worse, the valleys became too narrow for us to reverse course and fly out of the bad weather. We'd have to continue for at least another thirty minutes before flying out of the mountains. It became dangerous and unfortunately, self-induced. Thank goodness our highly experienced navigators focused on their instruments and didn't panic. We cut the mission short after clearing the mountains, clouds, and turbulence.

During that first year, vastly more challenging missions included terrain-following flight profiles, forward area refuelings, and blacked-out landings. They honed my flying skills to what I hoped would validate a level of credibility with the younger and incredibly talented pilots. Our mission partners, the guys we carried in the back of the plane, remained secretive and at the top of their game. I found a good routine. Life never remains the same for long. Things change.

Lt Col Sylvester got orders and several weeks later Lt Col Talkalot showed up. He'd become the new Squadron Commander and I'd fill his Director of Operations position. I liked him. He'd been a key planner for Operation Just

Cause, the 1989 invasion of Panama to depose general and dictator Manuel Noriega.

The leadership situation began faltering when Lt Col Talkalot delayed his qualification checkout. It soon became obvious that he lacked the requisite confidence to navigate the MC-130E. In fairness, the position demanded a great deal of recent experience and skill. Only exceptional navigators could multi-task under extreme stress and still operate the highly complex equipment. His trepidation didn't come without reason. The Group Director of Operations ordered Lt Col Talkalot to complete his check ride within the month … to this day I question a conversation I had with our Chief of Standardization and Evaluation.

I asked the evaluator to prepare a basic check ride, to discuss emergencies before the flight so that Lt Col Talkalot could deal with an in-flight version of the same thing without screwing it up. I promised that he'd never fly without a strong instructor next to him. Never before had I so much as hinted at giving a "soft" flight check. But I did it that day. I hadn't thought of Lt Col Talkalot as a crew member. A commander led and he didn't necessarily fly. He'd never fly another actual combat mission. He only needed to understand it. The conversation still tightens my stomach muscles. I'll never forget it.

Several months later, Lt Col Talkalot changed assignments and moved to an office within 13th Air Force. I assumed command of the 1st Special Operations Squadron. The change came with a mixed bag of emotions. I felt like I'd come in through the back door after failing to keep Lt Col Talkalot afloat. On the other hand, the opportunity brought a deep feeling of honor. The unit bore a rich heritage since its inception as the 1st Pursuit Squadron. The newly formed 353rd Special Operations Group leadership team became an incredible team with Col Leon "Papasan" Hess as Commander and Col Dave Miles as Director of Operations. The men of the 1st SOS stood as professionals, good at what they did, a fun-loving group, and a family.

Lt Col Onnie "Wayne-O" Owens became my Director of Operations. Wayne brought a wealth of corporate knowledge to the table and I'm sure that's why he'd been selected for the position. It felt like a great team during unusual times.

Chapter 28

Innovation distinguishes between a leader and a follower.
– Steve Jobs

I NEEDED CONSIDERABLE PRACTICE TO BECOME proficient at aerial refueling. In a pinch, I could get plugged into a KC-135 or KC-10 tanker and hold on long enough to get gas. Aerial refueling didn't require incredible skill when the air remained clear and calm, but it became more challenging at night, in bad weather, and with turbulence. It seemed unnatural to fly within feet of another very large aircraft and felt like flying underneath it when transferring fuel. Like many things, aerial refueling became much easier with practice. I never did get enough of it.

I found myself scheduled for a refueling mission and flew through clear blue skies to the pre-contact position behind the tanker. Everything looked perfect and I anticipated a good training session.

"Do you know you have a big hole in your wing?" the Boomer called over the radio.

We looked out the window and yikes! Mid-wing along the leading edge I noticed a two-foot diameter hole. I turned to the Instructor Pilot.

"We've gotten this far without any problems. Can we please just get a little gas before going home?"

"Nope."

We made a U-turn and headed home. Opportunity lost.

Formed aircrews created meaningful aircrew patches, which they wore when deployed on exercises. I loved the fact that a lot of thought went into their design … except perhaps Muffin-Man's crew patch that featured a naked blonde sitting on the top of an MC-130 aircraft. A Kingdom of Thailand general officer directed the patch not to be displayed in his country, and if he saw it again the aircrew would be deported.

An alternative to wearing customized crew patches also existed, going without patches on certain missions. While missions occasionally required aircrew to remove patches, they most often did not.

To increase the consciousness of operational security, I came up with a patch plan. Long tactical missions led to talking of mission details at street-side bars and that often exposed more operational activity than wanted. I created an innocent diversion.

First, I designed a random patch and titled it the Arizona National Guard. Next, I ordered several hundred from a local patch-making shop. Each deploying crewmember took a patch and would talk about the Arizona National Guard rather than rehashing the recent mission details. It confused everyone, and I'm not sure anyone learned the lesson about lax operational security. Worse, Special Operations Command, Pacific caught wind of it and decided I'd instigated tactical deception without them pre-approving it. I received a verbal hand-slap and hoped the generals found my misguided initiative more laughable than threatening.

Skippy Carson might best be described as a human anomaly. He impressed me as being quite smart but at the same time capable of formulating head-scratching ideas. His occasional nerd-like look could change in a moment to something more serious. As a Talon II navigator, he mastered the art of multi-tasking under incredibly stressful situations. His job included keeping the rest of us from banging into craggy mountain cliffs while flying 250 feet above some remote valley floor … in bad weather while the Electronic Warfare Officer called out airborne threats and announced, "Break left!" or "Break right!" This is the same Skippy who hosted one of the most memorable housewarming parties on Clark Air Base.

A festive mood complemented by an assortment of balloons clinging to the ceiling took root. Drinks flowed freely, guests overflowed onto the front lawn where war stories came to life. I should mention that compressed hydrogen can be procured for less than compressed oxygen in the Philippines so filling the balloons with hydrogen didn't raise concerns. Out of the blue, the house nearly exploded from the concussion. Skippy had jokingly poked one of the balloons with his cigarette.

The blast dazed him, knocking his glasses sideways. His hair always appeared a bit disheveled but now it looked spiky amidst a cloud of smoke that clung to his head. He resembled a young, confused Einstein emerging from a nearly demolished building.

We did incredible things most others only dreamed about, like landing on foreign highways in the middle of the night. We flew thousands of miles on a clandestine and dangerous mission before being turned around and learning it'd been another practice run. We planned missions that we knew had a less than-even chance of returning and hoped like hell we'd never get tasked to fly them.

It seemed Manila existed on the verge of another coup attempt. The U.S. military usually distanced itself from such things and when a coup attempt actually did happen, I found myself holed up with an aircrew in Bangkok. We carried a team of specialized folks with us so returning to Manila needed to wait a few days. I remember briefing the aircrew on how peaceful things would look from the air, at least until bullets "pinged" the aircraft as they zipped through the interior. This time the descent and landing happened uneventfully. On other training missions, we occasionally returned to base with bullet holes in the airframe.

Between the endless trips throughout Asia, I decided to look at operations more strategically, to develop a daily rhythm that better prepared us for future taskings, and planned to fashion a training regime that supported the evolving nature of nation-building, foreign internal defense, and basic military-to-military relationships. Bigger things interrupted my strategic planning.

July 16, 1990. The building shook and continued to shake. Those few still at work poked heads out of offices and in unison thought about getting under a desk. As a group, we ran for the building exit. From the parking lot, we watched buildings roll up and down as if floating on the ocean. The earthquake lasted for almost a minute before things returned to normal.

We awaited damage assessments and suspected we'd be tasked with some sort of support. The quake rumbled at seven-point-seven intensity and originated near Cabanatuan City. The most destructive jolts occurred in the heavily populated mountain city of Baguio. Hotels, factories, and university buildings collapsed, twenty-eight in all. Mountain roads leading to Baguio disappeared in landslides. Electricity went out, water lines bent or split, and communications became disrupted. It'd be days before rescue forces arrived in the stricken area.

I awoke at 3 a.m. for the next ten days and flew one of our MC-130s to San Fernando, La Union's municipal airport. We departed before dawn loaded with as much fuel as possible and landed at San Fernando before other aircraft filled the limited open space. Our mission included parking in the far corner of the postage-stamp-sized tarmac and refueling rescue helicopters.

The maximum number of C-130s considered safe to occupy the tarmac at any given time totaled one. I counted six of them crammed together. Between ten and twenty private aircraft occupied the tarmac and as many as twenty helicopters sat in the adjoining grassy areas. It appeared about as packed as packed can be.

Two or three times during the day, an HC-130 landed and taxied as close as possible to our aircraft. The loadmasters uncoiled hoses between the aircraft and refilled our tanks. We continued refueling the rescue helicopters. This continued until sunset when we flew back to Clark Air Base for the night. The scenario repeated itself over and over again.

I flew to Baguio one afternoon onboard a Marine H-53 helicopter. As we approached Baguio's runway, I saw a huge chasm slicing across the entire width of the runway. It appeared to be three to five feet wide and looked very, very deep.

The earthquake killed nearly sixteen hundred people. At least eighty hotel employees and guests died when the Hyatt Terraces Baguio Hotel collapsed. Rescue teams pulled three hotel employees from the rubble nearly two weeks later.

One Air Force Pararescueman amputated a leg deep within the rubble before extracting another survivor. San Fernando's refueling operations generated a sense of urgency and purpose. Baguio existed in a far more brutal reality.

Short of war, I couldn't imagine anything worse than what I experienced in Baguio. Less than a year later, Mt. Pinatubo interrupted our routine, and life took another turn …

Chapter 29

The measure of who we are is what we do with what we have.
– Vince Lombardi

Tuesday, June 11, 1991 Stars and Stripes

APRIL IN THE PHILIPPINES BLESSED US WITH the best weather of the year. Each night brought a cool evening freshness that comforted everyone until the sun's warmth displaced it. One morning, I noticed white puffs of steam seeping from the jagged featureless mountains west of Clark Air Base. What appeared to be an innocent anomaly would, over the next months, develop into hell on earth and I'd soon find myself in the middle of it.

Manila Bulletin writers often wrote dramatic prose while skimping on the factual background. Their alarming concerns about Mt. Pinatubo's seeming return to life sounded dramatic but raised few eyebrows. When the *Pacific*

Stars & Stripes wrote similar warnings, my eyebrows raised. The hair on my neck tingled.

Mt. Pinatubo existed as a nondescript peak of 5,741 feet located eight-point-two miles west of Clark Air Base and twenty-two miles north of U.S. Naval Base Subic Bay. It sat in the backyard of both. Those who followed the local news more closely put things into a palatable perspective by suggesting that most of the venting occurred on the far side of the ridgeline. Writers inferred that any eruption would affect the sleepy town of Iba and those other communities on the opposite side of the mountains from Clark. To me, the slopes appeared anything but menacing. They remained placid and lush with deep green vegetation.

A Philippine seismology team installed vibration-sensing gadgetry during May, mostly atop nearby slopes. They readily admitted that predicting when a volcano vented or exploded remained at best a very imprecise science. I listened intently to their best-case and worst-case scenarios during Crisis Action Team presentations for the senior military leadership. General Willie Studer, the 13th Air Force commander, and his colonels understandably focused on the worst case. They conceived a master volcano evacuation plan after several weeks ... that spiraled a bit out of control and in some ways appeared quite short-sighted.

Volcano Conditions of Readiness, or VOLCONs, consisted of five levels of danger with VOLCON I being the worst case. At VOLCON II (high danger) we'd begin an orderly evacuation of the base.

Unbeknownst to the military planners, volcanologists already had established VOLCON levels from years earlier. Enter Murphy's Law, or perhaps a corollary about confusion. The military and civilian VOLCONs now increased in opposite directions. Many military families listened to the Armed Forces Philippine Network (AFPN) radio station and heard the military levels. Quite a few, however, also listened to local Filipino radio stations that announced readiness condition changes independently and always ahead of AFPN's broadcasts. They also changed in the opposite direction.

May 13th, volcanologist interview.

> An earthquake swarm with 30-180 earthquakes per day occurred. Sulfur dioxide levels have risen, an indication there is fresh magma rising under the surface.

On May 28th they announced sulfur dioxide emissions had again increased drastically compared to two weeks earlier.

Yet everything in the mountains looked normal enough and the military assessment reflected a cautious, but calm situation. Local reporters, on the other hand, began painting a more ominous picture.

As commander of the 1st Special Operations Squadron, I felt compelled to communicate what I knew to the families of my squadron members. On Thursday, June 6th I gathered everyone in the squadron briefing room for an official update. I dispelled a rumor that we lived in a death zone even though we could easily be in a very dangerous location. Some believed the whole thing might be a hoax. It wasn't.

Col Stankovich, our Group Vice Commander, explained the nature of the volcano lurking in our backyard. Mt.

Pinatubo fits the explosive category, unlike the Hawaiian lava-flow type. He mentioned that when Mt. St. Helens exploded, its eruption created a pyroclastic flow, a hot ash cloud that could travel as fast as two hundred miles per hour and toast or collapse everything in its path. Yikes! Fortunately, a pyroclastic flow never did reach the base, although three-thousand-degree ash did get within a mile of the western boundary. We unanimously decided the situation appeared to be serious.

Warm air and blue skies greeted me on Sunday morning as I rode my scooter to the Command Post for a status update. Based on whatever volcano restrictions might be forthcoming, I'd review and adjust the upcoming week's flying schedule. Shortly after I arrived, an unannounced Crisis Action Team meeting convened.

The room buzzed with enthusiastic banter about producing a volcano brochure, the ongoing seismic samplings, and the prospect of conducting an orderly evacuation to Subic Bay. Evacuation? I perked up when General Studer and Col Jeff Grimes, the 3rd Tactical Fighter Wing commander, referred to Clark AB as "the only military base in the world with a volcano evacuation plan …" and touted their plan for "… the greatest peacetime evacuation ever to take place."

This didn't sound good. An evacuation now seemed inevitable.

What did they know that I didn't?

It seemed like a good idea to gather the aircrew and brief them on the heightened potential for evacuation. I'd get it organized as soon as the meeting concluded. Later that day crews flew three MC-130s and four large helicopters twenty-five miles southwest to Naval Air Station Cubi Point. Maintainers had disassembled an additional C-130 that had been flown from Elmendorf Air Force Base in Alaska to Clark Air Base for a major inspection. It required significant reassembly before being flown. I returned home from the morning command post visit shortly after midnight on Sunday.

Activity increased and tensions grew. The aircrew who flew to Subic left their families behind at Clark. Wives with children, pets, house girls, gardeners, security guards, and so many other loose ends remained. Evacuating to the provinces would have been relatively easy for some families, but the military didn't offer it as an official option. Everyone would drive to Subic.

I worried about the Elmendorf C-130. If I simply ignored it because of its state of disassembly, it stood a good chance of being destroyed by the volcano.

"Let's try to get it flyable. Reconnect all the hydraulic lines and chain the landing gear in the down position. Let me know if there's any way to take off using all four engines and then immediately shut down the bad one once airborne."

We could have taken off using only three engines, and it would have been safer than the four-engine option, but it required a complicated waiver. We didn't have the luxury of waiting for that approval.

The phone rang. Another wife with questions. As soon as I hung up, it rang again, and again. I packed a small, incomplete bag and made a quick video of our clothing, furniture, and electronics before pulling open the refrigerator door and looking for a beer. The phone rang again – another question about what to pack. I grabbed the first of three San Miguel beers, then another, and then the last. Two hours after falling asleep my wife woke me and grabbed a few last toiletries before departing for temporary refuge at the home of the Korean Attaché and his wife. I headed back to work.

We left too early to inform Carmen, our faithful house girl, that we'd evacuated. She'd be on her own.

June 10th, volcanologists report.

> Sulfur dioxide started to escape again. The dome has become unstable and has created the first hot pyroclastic flows which have been accompanied by larger ash eruptions. Evacuations are in full swing to move people out of the twelve-point-five-mile danger zone.

Vehicles at Clark AB before departing for Subic Bay NB

The evacuation of Clark Air Base quickly blossomed into a gargantuan undertaking. A total of 14,400 military members and their families stuffed valuables and compact belongings into ragtag "Clark mobiles" and began snaking their way along well-marked country roads toward Subic Bay. Derelict car after car inched along bumper-to-bumper. The procession averaged six hours over a distance that normally took one hour and fifteen minutes.

It felt every bit a steamy ninety-five degrees. Owners watched as vehicles overheated and abandoned others after they gasped their last breaths. In all cases, they kept moving. Most vehicles found Subic Bay only to queue for limited parking. Accountability, processing, and assignment of quarters seemed equally overwhelming.

Evacuating Clark AB geographically rather than by military unit seemed like a wise decision when staff officers concocted the plan. However, problems surfaced as soon as people showed up at Subic and Corpsmen assigned them to quarters willy-nilly. Squadrons lost contact with their personnel. Most people did not have cellphones and the resulting lack of organizational connectivity became a major issue.

Evacuees very quickly inundated the Navy staff. It became a long, tedious day for all involved.

I watched the mass automotive exodus from the far end of Clark's flight line and thanked the gods that I'd be occupied flying what turned out to be three shuttles between Clark Air Base and Naval Air Station Cubi Point. My last flight terminated at Cubi Point so I never did join those driving cars. One of the smarter things I thought to do involved loading my 250c.c. scooter onto the last aircraft.

The loadmasters conveniently overlooked the requirement for a complex Hazardous Declaration form that addressed the scooter's fuel and battery. At least I'd have transportation at Subic.

Sometimes things happen at exactly the wrong time. Before all the evacuation activities got into full swing, one of my dental fillings cracked and fell out. As odd as it seemed for my tooth to crack the day before a major evacuation, it seemed equally odd to find a Naval flight-line dental clinic located next to our operations, to walk in, and to get treated. I remember the dentist asking if he needed to remove me from flying status because of the Novocain he'd injected.

They can't ground me now. Think of something ...

I told him the USAF had recently changed the rules on this and grounding me wouldn't be necessary.

Chapter 30

Earn your leadership every day.
– Michael Jordan

I PROCEEDED TO THE CUBI BACHELOR Officer's Quarters (BOQ) with a slightly sinister feeling at having remained on flight status. My Director of Operations got the word out that we'd conduct an operations call near the BOQ pool area. It remained critically important for me to know how many flyers could be assembled and formed into crews. I sensed that a disaster resided on our doorstep and we'd eventually be tasked with some sort of relief mission.

At 9 a.m. I made a few comments before gasping as a huge mushroom-shaped cloud rose over the heads of those assembled in front of me. Mt. Pinatubo had finally blown! I got to the point.

"Go to your quarters and get into your flight suits, get your professional gear, and then commandeer whatever transportation you can find to get to the aircraft."

This amounted to a challenging undertaking since most of the enlisted crewmembers now lived thirty to forty-five minutes away in Barrio Barreto and no one had vehicles.

June 12, 1991. Ash reached 12.5 miles above Mt. Pinatubo

Our four aircraft sat in various stages of preparation on the Upper Carrier Deck. The area included a large asphalt tarmac on the opposite side of the runway from the main airport where it jutted out into the ocean. What appeared to be a disorganized hub of activity amounted to just that. Maintenance wrench-benders and aircrew arrived randomly and instinctively joined others in prepping the aircraft. I directed our crews to wait until they had, as a minimum, a pilot, co-pilot, engineer, and loadmaster before starting engines. I'd provide further instructions before they launched.

The mushroom cloud from earlier continued to grow and expand at the upper levels. It looked exactly like a nuclear explosion. There'd been no atomic rush of hot air, no noise, and no sudden ash fall. However, it came to life with ominous and awesome power. Its dark roiling ash-laden clouds clawed their way to more than eighty thousand feet.

We launched four C-130s, including the 3-engine plane from Alaska, and three MH-53J helicopters toward Villamor

Air Base, which shared its runways with Ninoy Aquino International Airport in Manila. How strange that Manila existed only forty miles away yet everything there remained normal. The sense of foreboding that gripped our souls at Subic Bay didn't exist here. It felt more than a little weird. By 3 p.m. we'd received reports that very little ash had fallen on NAS Cubi Point and that prevailing winds carried the remainder well out to sea.

"Let's head back." And off we went.

Once back in the danger zone, we secured the aircraft and headed to quarters. I found the senior staff at DJs, a casual bar attached to our billeting facility. After several games of table-top shuffleboard, a frantic call from the flight line came in. The C-130H from Alaska had broken its towing attachment bracket and currently obstructed the only taxiway between the parking area and the runway. As luck would have it, I found myself to be technically the only pilot qualified to fly it mostly because of its slightly different starting procedures. Until I could start the engines and move the aircraft, it'd block any other aircraft from taxiing to the runway. That'd be a major problem should the volcano erupt again.

I grabbed another pilot and together with a maintenance crew chief, cranked engines, taxied to a run-up area, and re-indexed the malfunctioning prop controller. This would, hopefully, bring the propeller gearbox into normal operating ranges. Our maintenance actions proved unsuccessful, although we ultimately relocated the airplane to a better spot. It felt late although I had no idea of the time. I fell asleep within seconds of lowering my head to the pillow.

The phone rang twenty minutes later, and I received word to scramble the fleet. There'd been another large eruption.

June 13, 1991 notes from a newscaster.

> Ash eruptions increase, even more, creating a plume reaching 15.5 miles elevation. This happens after a short pause of twenty-six hours without explosions. Seismicity remains extremely high.

Darkness prevailed. We telephoned notifications to the aircrews, most of whom stayed miles away in Barrio Barretto. The flight line once again became a beehive of activity. Maintenance crew chiefs scurried through aircraft preflights, removed dust covers from engine intakes, and pulled safety pins. This time we'd identify an airborne holding point out over the ocean, stack all aircraft in that area, and wait for the ash fall to clear. I pulled aside a pilot and a navigator and explained what I needed. Two other crews had to be told not to taxi until they either gathered all their crew members or until I reversed that order. One aircrew consisted of a young pilot in the left seat and a crew chief in the engineer's seat. He told me they could go, except they didn't have a co-pilot, navigator, engineer, radio operator, electronic warfare officer, or loadmaster. Another crew declared themselves ready to launch even though they lacked an engineer and loadmaster.

I told them to sit tight until a loadmaster showed up. They launched twenty minutes later with all their required crew members.

The ashfall avoidance plan seemed flawed from the git-go. It placed four C-130s and three helicopters in a tightly stacked holding pattern right in the middle of numerous looming thunderstorms. The first aircraft to depart planned to take the lower altitude because it'd also be the first to land later in the night. But this required the later departures to climb through already occupied airspace. Menacing lightning flashes prompted an immediate revision. We relocated inland and set up a fifty-mile south-to-north holding pattern that placed us approximately fifteen miles upwind of Mt Pinatubo. We flew that pattern for four hours as we inhaled the "rotten eggs" smell of sulfur each time we passed the volcano.

The earlier engine run on the C-130H didn't resolve the propeller problem, and not unexpectedly, the number four prop began surging out of limits shortly after take-off. Normally, I'd never have flown in this condition, but this unusual circumstance of leaving the aircraft on the ground could easily have caused its total demise. I also had the landing gear chained in the down position and that limited our airspeed.

The most exciting part about flying the aircraft with only three engines involved flying a very steep four-point-three-degree glideslope each time we returned to Cubi Point. It also required focus to keep the aircraft in the middle of the runway when reversing engines. By the time we'd landed, our bodies wanted to shut down. We needed time to get some sleep. We felt exhausted. At the same time, we knew that when the next alert sounded we'd be ready to go. I got five hours of much-needed sleep.

I read a clipping about the Aeta tribesmen who lived near the top of Mt. Pinatubo and how they harbored concerns about eruptions occurring as a result of their decision to start sacrificing chickens rather than pigs. Because of their declining living conditions, pigs had become too expensive to be used as sacrificial offerings. Several years earlier they'd replaced pigs with chickens. Our beliefs couldn't have been further apart, yet we all suffered the same consequence of the eruptions. At this point, the "why" didn't particularly matter.

Reports of another major eruption crackled from the UHF satellite communications radio. Tremors and earthquakes increased in frequency and intensity. Approximately three hundred tremors occurred daily with seismic evidence of growing instability within the mountain. Our Special Operations Group Commander directed the evacuation of our aircraft to Kadena Air Base in Okinawa, Japan. The helos would be moved into hangars and prepped for possible disaster relief taskings. The aircraft would depart with augmented aircrews and maintenance technicians. The families of those service members would remain under the shadow of the volcano.

Master Sergeant Joel Kay, the squadron's First Shirt, expressed concern about the communications link between Subic "Bat Cave Ops" and the remaining enlisted personnel hunkered down at various locations in Barrio Barreto. He relocated stragglers into the Marmont Resort Hotel where most of the enlisted families already resided. It turned out to be a very wise decision.

Chapter 31

The power of a volcano when it erupts is so evident, so visible, so palpable.
– Werner Herzog

JUNE 15, 1991 NOTES FROM A NEWSCASTER.

Mount Pinatubo is now erupting continuously. It's shooting up faster than the ash column can rise, so the column collapses, raining tons and tons of ash and rock fragments all over Pampanga, switching off the sun like a light bulb and plunging the province into total darkness. It's so dark you can't see your hand stretched out in front of you, and the ashfall is so thick even sound waves can't pass through. Thus, everything is muffled. You have to strain your ear to hear a conversation, like a movie with the volume turned low. The remaining soldiers at Clark Air Base watch the darkness creep across the parade ground, like an evil cloud or the angel of death shutting out every street lamp, porch light, car light, and flashlight that stands in the way. In Mabalacat, residents see it as a solid black curtain being drawn down from the sky. They go out to the street mesmerized by the sight of pumice pebbles falling from the sky and pelting house roofs and car tops, followed by a rain of mud, then sand. The rain doubles the weight of sand and soon tree branches crack, coconut trees fold like umbrellas, and house roofs start caving in.

Photo by Alberto Garcia captures the immensity of the moment.

Typhoon Yunga brewed off the east coast of Luzon, and by 9:00 a.m. on Saturday, it moved directly overhead Subic. The significance of the typhoon involved its winds carrying most of Pinatubo's ash directly to Subic and only then back toward Clark.

June 15, 1991 notes from a newscaster.

> While typhoon Yunga passes 47 miles NE of Pinatubo, causing heavy rainfall and lahar to race down the volcano at twenty miles per hour, the largest explosion starts in mid-morning at 10:27 a.m. It lasts nine hours and spews more than 1.2 cubic miles of magma. The eruption column reaches an incredible twenty-two-mile height and encircles the globe in the stratosphere.

A voice crackled across the SATCOM announcing another eruption, an explosive blast that launched seven cubic miles of earth fifty thousand feet into the sky. Winds carried much of it in our direction. By 10 a.m., my world turned darker than dark.

Not only weird, but it also happened at 10 a.m. in total darkness.

Ash particulate fell so thick that not an iota of sunlight penetrated it. All illumination disappeared except for sparking telephone insulators and the ensuing explosive flashes as faltering transformers shorted. What happened next comprised the most bizarre, eerie, frightening experience of my life.

Darkness became absolute ... black ... darkness like being in a sealed closet without light. Trembling earthquakes made everyone want to get outside to safety. Except, the outside appeared dark, inky dark, and shrouded in a surrealistic electrical storm with blizzard-like ash swirling from the sky. Volcanic ash provided the perfect conduit for an amazing electrical display. Jagged bolts of electricity sought paths of least resistance across the sky and lingered unbroken before disappearing into black. Background flashes sequenced in reddish-orange. I felt afloat in a nightmarish dream.

Everyone's sense of feel shook with the earthquakes, while visually the unusual lightning discharges spiked an already unnatural sky. Familiar sounds of thunder mixed with the sounds of tree limbs snapping and then splattering seconds later on the jungle floor. It all echoed with an unearthly stereo effect. Random radio transmissions signaling emergencies across Subic's expanse interrupted the frenzied noises of nature at its worst.

From late morning through the early evening, radio calls crackled more frequently. I received an alarming notification from MSgt Kay that three buildings had collapsed across the street from the Marmont Resort Hotel. Three airmen became injured, one of them a member of the 1st Special Operations Squadron. More buildings collapsed … the Hill Top Club, the gymnasium, the Chief Petty Officer's Club, and many, many more. Altogether, well over two hundred buildings caved in during the night. Ash-laden ships in the harbor became top-heavy and unstable. Seamen desperately shoveled tons of ash overboard.

Volcanic ash as heavy as wet sand eventually caused structural collapse.

At the Marmont, a late-night hell unfolded. Many of the dependents had seen their husbands evacuate airplanes the day prior and found themselves on their own trying to survive. MSgt Kay and others established a field hospital in the hotel lobby. Some of the men gathered the children and tried to soothe their fears while wives teetered on the verge of hysteria. Other sergeants organized work crews to shovel accumulated ash from the hotel's roof. Their efforts saved lives and prevented greater structural damage than had already occurred.

We moved our poolside command center at NAS Cubi Point inside DJ's slot machine room. Throughout the night we heard call after call for help. We'd also heard official updates on the deteriorating situation including the crisis in Barrio Barreto. A multi-purpose all-terrain utility vehicle, more commonly known as HMMWV, would drive to Barrio Barreto. A small team would assess the situation first-hand, provide limited relief, and determine the best rescue course of action. It'd depart Subic within an hour and I immediately decided to be in that vehicle when it departed. I stepped into the dark wearing combat boots, shorts, a t-shirt, and a bandana and began jogging toward the Sampaguita Club. That's where I'd help direct the rescue effort.

As I ran through the ongoing ash blizzard, visibility became abysmal, not more than 150 feet. Along my jungle descent toward the coastal roadway, I came upon a Marine Quonset hut with lights inside. I clamored through the door.

"Can someone give me a flashlight?" I coughed out.

A young Marine gave me his and I disappeared back into the storm. The run continued, just over six miles, and my eyes filled with ash to the point of near blindness. I lost track of the road and ended up face-to-face with three tug boats. The main road existed behind me somewhere! Then I spotted a line of telephone poles and knew they also marked where the road should be. Each step felt like jogging along a sandy beach with six inches of soft sand. Branches continuously snapped loose and crashed nearby. My veins ran hot with adrenaline until I finally pushed through Sampaguita's doors looking like the abominable sandman.

Unfortunately, someone with more sense than me deemed the mission too dangerous, and as a result, the HMMWV never left for Barrio Barreto. I worried about the families but could do nothing at this point. I returned to the storm and set a slower pace jogging back up the mountain ridge to NAS Cubi Point.

The sounds of imminent structural failure echoed through the Marmont Hotel. MSgt Kay and several others risked life and limb going door to door in dark hallways to get everyone out. Once free of the unsafe structure they trudged down ash-filled streets toward another hotel called the Sea Breeze. During the trek, the women and children passed crushed bodies in the street, endured further earthquakes, and became drenched in wet, gritty ash.

Morning arrived with a glimmer of daylight. The six hundred stranded dependents at the Sea Breeze felt drained. They'd spent much of the previous night either outside in the wet ash or inside the Sea Breeze lobby. High adrenaline levels subsided and fatigue set in. Eventually, several buses bounced and chugged their way along ash-rutted roads and rescued the tired, scared survivors.

Back on Subic, we assessed the overall physical damage, which appeared to be significant. Simple survival became a real issue. Electricity wouldn't be restored for days or weeks, and we found ourselves without fresh water. We possessed no phones and very little food. Worse, no immediate relief seemed possible.

Survivors hunkered down throughout the area and we needed to bring them together somehow. Most found a new home in the jet engine shop where they'd been issued cots and a couple of Meals Ready to Eat, commonly called MREs. It looked like a turn-of-the-century sweatshop with wall-to-wall cots surrounding heavy equipment, wet floors, women looking frazzled, children playing quietly, or crying, bare light bulbs dangling from a ceiling wire, low illumination, professional spit-and-shine airmen with two-day beard growths, and pervasive exhaustion.

Despite the austere surroundings, someone found a generator and strung more lights, and best of all, got a fan working. An ex-Army Special Forces Sergeant by the name of George Fails rigged a natural shower from a nearby mountain creek by fashioning a split bamboo aqueduct. Music from a Manila radio station twanged in the background. Life returned to a bearable level for the time being.

Real shakers and lesser earthquakes occurred every day. I sensed they routinely surpassed 5.5 on the Richter scale. Each morning between 3 a.m. and 4 a.m., the earth jolted and rocked with a low-grade rumble similar to a train in the distance. I listened for structural snaps or crackles and decided that if I heard anything like crumbling concrete I'd open a window and jump from my third-floor room onto the piles of ash below. I woke up every morning at 3 a.m. for the next six months awaiting that same low-frequency rumble.

Chapter 32

Remind me that the most fertile lands were built by the fires of volcanoes.
– Andrea Gibson

DEPENDENTS EVACUATED ON A FIRST-COME, first-out basis after which all non-essential Air Force active-duty members left. This process introduced quite a few unforeseen issues. The segregated evacuations caused serious and mostly unnecessary stress. Filipino wives traveled with children, animals, and bags to a strange land where they'd be met by unknown relatives in a world they didn't fully understand. Their military husbands most often followed a week or two later.

Out-processing became a nightmarish all-day experience. Accountability of people remained at the core of processing, while tedious legal and financial details took time and generated incredibly long lines. We kept an eye on those in line for signs of heatstroke and dehydration. The single most critical resource throughout the evacuation time frame immediately became potable water because all the normal water outlets had been destroyed. When the MV 1st Lt Jack Lummus docked, it desalinated seawater. But after two days, its filters became so clogged with ash that the ship had to relocate to deep water before it could restart the purification process. Oddly, we found a single potable water outlet just outside our Quonset hut. It dispensed water directly from an off-base reservoir. Two of our maintenance sergeants requisitioned several water mules, which functioned as large mobile water containers We filled and deployed them to the processing area. Repositioning the mules from the water outlet to the other side of the base required a slow, bumpy ride along extremely deformed and pot-holed roadways.

Evacuees board the USS Abraham Lincoln before departing for Cebu.

The departure sequence began when a family arrived at one of the car parking areas and boarded a shuttle bus headed for the Sampaguita Club. They carried all their belongings, including suitcases, boxes, strollers, children, and pets. They held these everywhere they went until they arrived in the United States.

The Sampaguita Club became anything but a pleasant place. It remained dark, very hot, and humid with a smothering musty odor inside. After having passports and visas validated, evacuees were manifested and told to proceed to the gymnasium across the parking lot. For those who didn't have the correct documents, staffers took administrative shortcuts to allow authorized individuals to continue onward.

The line to the gymnasium always appeared long and either incredibly hot or incredibly exposed to rain. I watched drenched women and children with suitcases and animal cages mired in ash mud and water. A final legal and financial review occurred inside the gym, and with good timing, dependents soon boarded buses for transportation to a ship. If they timed it wrong, they'd move to a common area and wait for the next ship to arrive before loading.

The Navy processed Naval personnel differently. Everyone with a valid ID card quickly boarded without administrative processing. Processing personnel completed that requirement during the twenty-four-hour cruise to Cebu. However, because the initial screening had been so cursory, more than a few girlfriends and extended family members made it to Cebu before being discovered and returned to Luzon. It seemed the Navy's approach moved vastly quicker and inflicted less pain.

Dogs and cats required special care and handling. Many dependents brought their pets to Subic but left them behind when boarding an evacuation ship. Initially, all animals found temporary shelter in the basement parking garage at the Cubi Point Bachelor Officer's Quarters. We issued a large triple-wall box for each animal. Owners cut holes into the sides for the animals to see out and breathe fresh air. I assigned two airmen the full-time job of feeding the dogs and cats each day. They walked the dogs each morning as well. The love and care shown to the shell-shocked critters made a big difference. One of us also made arrangements with the installation veterinarian to inoculate all of the animals and provide them with health certificates for their journey back to the States. Those abandoned pets without an identified owner mostly found new homes nearby.

A combat bath felt unbelievably refreshing even if it only happened once a week.

With the dependents gone, we found ourselves working eighteen-hour days. After missing my weekly combat shower and not having done laundry, I smelled unacceptably bad. It seemed time for a visit to the beach where I'd attempt to clean everything in the ocean. After wading out chest-deep I declared my cleanup plan a failure. The concentration of ash in the water felt like liquid sandpaper. Making matters worse, as I approached the water my identification badge fell from my uniform onto the beach. Hours later, a Security Police patrol noticed my footprints leading into the ocean and then discovered my badge. They assumed I'd made a one-way trip. The next day someone gasped with relief when seeing me still alive. We shared a good laugh before informing the SPs that a further search would not be required.

On June 29, I boarded a 17th Special Operations Squadron HC-130 and flew to Okinawa. My 250c.c. scooter hid securely under a tarp in the cargo compartment and we never bothered with the necessary paperwork to bring it into Japan. After all, it had started life as a Yamaha.

Chapter 33

Learn from the mistakes of others. You won't live long enough to make all of them yourself.
– Unknown.

ADJUSTING TO OPERATIONS AT KADENA AIR Base, Okinawa, came with its share of unusual challenges. The entire contingent of several hundred airmen found themselves separated from their families and housed in temporary quarters. Our undetermined duty assignment status made buying a car difficult. Something as simple as getting to work became a daily challenge.

Work ... the abandoned Aero Club building found unforeseen usefulness when engineers delayed its demolition so we could occupy it until finding another building. Our floor space barely surpassed that of the Base Theater's restroom. I ordered the flyers to remain in temporary quarters unless scheduled to fly or required for other essential duties. Everyone stressed.

One Engineer's displaced son in the United States became suicidal. A navigator couldn't locate his wife after she'd quietly boarded a ship at Subic Bay and relocated to the U.S. A maintenance technician turned into a pyromaniac and eventually got caught attempting to burn down his dormitory.

I consulted with our unit Flight Surgeon, Major Yamakawa, each evening to discuss aircrew stress levels. He kept me apprised of who he judged fit to fly and who needed a break. Little by little, Air Force Personnel reassigned squadron members to the U.S. and identified replacements.

The new folks would start showing up once our temporary status shifted to permanent.

My dog and cat remained in a stateside kennel until I finally got reassigned. Had I known the process would take almost seven months, I'd have found some alternative for housing the pets. As it turned out, the boarding bill climbed to seven thousand dollars! We arrived in Japan as disaster evacuees in June 1991 and remained in temporary status until the following February. I needed a change.

The Air Force considered reassigning me to the Air Force Special Operations Command Headquarters in Florida. My promotion potential looked quite good and the area supported a large retirement community. It sounded good.

At the same time, I realized that the U.S. military had just lost a major strategic basing option with the departure from Clark Air Base and Subic Bay Naval Base. I felt that a well-placed Air Force officer in the Joint U.S. Military Assistance Group Philippines, or USJUSMAG-PHIL, might influence the Mutual Defense Treaty to allow for future training access. The job would be a career-killer but it'd be meaningful and more importantly, less stressful. That'd be my next and last assignment.

JUSMAG-PHIL resided within Seafront Compound in the heart of Manila. The U.S. Embassy sat along Manila Bay several miles down Roxas Boulevard. As Chief of the Air Force Branch, I occupied a World War Two-era office complete with a Tagalog-speaking secretary in the adjoining room. I'd live in the high-rent district of Makati and fly a twin-engine King Air to tiny island destinations. These stretched from Ferdinand Marcos' Laoag International

Airport in northern Luzon to Tawi-Tawi in the Sulu Archipelago.

Col James "Nick" Rowe, my Army counterpart, had been assassinated several years earlier, and his death constantly reminded us of the potential for danger. We rode to and from work in armored SUVs and whether we liked it or not, had armed guards around us a lot of the time.

When not visiting Philippine military units throughout the islands, I researched and organized potential arms sales – UH-1 helicopters, OV-10 aircraft, and F-16s. I pushed the acquisition of a squadron of Navy A-4 fighters after a Middle East sale faltered. The administrative work proved exciting, but flying still held my heart.

One hot summer day, I flew toward a fast-building line of clouds while transiting from Cotabato City to Puerto Princessa. It looked like I'd pass over the clouds from a distance, but as luck would have it, they surged upward at the last moment like a huge roiling curtain rising before me. Whoa! Hard up, then down, wings dipped left and right, the autopilot kicked off, and just like that the aircraft broke into clear skies. Everything instantly returned to normal, except the windscreen now supported an inch of ice. I flew encased in ice for the next forty minutes before thawing out and landing on a steamy hot, humid runway.

Other flights proved to be far more fun than first imagined. One day a young Navy pilot and I flew several U.S. and Philippine colonels to San Fernando where we'd wait four to five hours before returning them to Manila.

As soon as they departed the airport for meetings, we changed into running togs and began a one-hour jog through the foothills. After returning to the aircraft, we changed into swimming suits, grabbed snorkels and masks, and hiked across the runway to the beach. A bangka boat owner happily motored us to a nearby coral reef. An hour or so later we returned to one of the nearby beach resorts, showered, and ordered a fresh seafood lunch.

No sooner had we hiked back to the aircraft and changed back into flight suits than the colonels appeared in a caravan of Jeep Cherokees. They apologized for taking so long and felt bad that we'd spent such a non-productive day waiting for them. I smiled.

"No problem Sir."

We flew a five-hour instrument and proficiency training mission each month. We'd depart Manila at 7 a.m. and fly to the mountainous destination of Baguio for breakfast. Climb-out featured a dramatic moment when passing approximately four thousand feet. That's normally where a temperature inversion held Manila's pollution. Crisp, clear skies suddenly engulfed us once we climbed through that layer. A feeling of warmth and goodness filled the cockpit. Baguio seemed an idyllic destination even though it presented one of the more difficult landings available to man.

The approach to landing under the best of conditions required preplanning and skill. Two miles from the runway the aircraft needed to skim over an intruding ridgeline. Pass it too high and the rest of the approach might as well have been engine out. The descent rate would be that high. Each end of the runway abruptly ended in sheer drop-offs. The runway had a significant slope and when landing downhill, stopping before going over the cliffs at the end of the runway became a real issue.

An older couple ran a quaint little bed and breakfast called Ruff House. As soon as they noticed our King Air, they'd come to the tarmac and greet us, accompany us to their restaurant, and serve us the world's best bacon and eggs. We loved talking with the friendly owners about all things Baguio. Next stop, Laoag International Airport.

Laoag is located in the northern portion of Luzon. This fell within Marcos's ancestral province and that appeared to be the only reason I could imagine such a large runway being built in this remote part of the country. We flew instrument approaches until doing them all several times and then headed home. San Fernando conveniently existed along our return route to Manila. We'd stop to refuel before walking to one of the beach resorts for a late lunch.

We flew over Manila Bay and followed visual landmarks to Ninoy Aquino International Airport's runway 13. The aviation authority considered it too short for the big commercial airliners, and as a result, it became available with minimal spacing delays. Clear fresh air transformed into congested, hazy, engine-revving street noise.

WALK RUN FLY

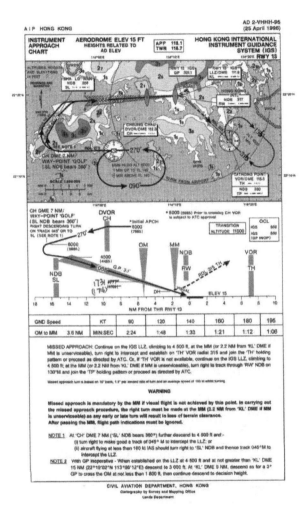

Hong Kong's Kai Tak Int'l Airport has a complex approach plate.

Hong Kong's Kai Tak International Airport ranked as The History Channel's 6th most dangerous airport in the world. It existed from 1925 until 1998. That's when Hong Kong Airport replaced it nineteen miles to the west. Pilots required a special checkout and I got mine during a late-night flight from Manila. Because of the geography with water on three sides of the runway and with Kowloon City's residential apartment complexes and towering mountains to the northeast of the airport, aircraft could not fly over the mountains and quickly drop in for a normal landing. Instead, aircraft had to fly above Victoria Harbour and Kowloon City, passing north of Mong Kok's Bishop Hill. This routing required tuning in several ADF beacons while monitoring multiple radio calls. Acute situational awareness became a critical element because of all the commercial aircraft being sequenced for the approach. Radio changes coupled with new headings and altitudes kept the cockpit busy and focused. After passing Bishop Hill, we transitioned to visual procedures, following spotlights atop high-rise apartments until identifying Checkerboard Hill. Its large red and white checkerboard sign marked our sharp turn to the final approach. Immediately before reaching the checkerboard, we spotted the runway forty-seven degrees to the right and started a descending turn toward it.

Hearing stories about Kai Tak didn't do it justice. Flying the approach in marginal weather at night provided a more vivid sense of aviation's extremes. Even then, landing a King Air had been relatively easy. Landing a Boeing 747 would have been vastly more challenging.

We also flew to more exotic places like Zamboanga, Jolo, and Tawi Tawi. Any time spent on the ground at these destinations required armed guards. Bombings in the local markets occurred regularly. Other locations such as Cotabato City, Davao, and Iligan City ranked as less threatening but still dangerous to those wearing a U.S.

uniform. It gave balance to our more routine flying while adding an exotic touch to the nights.

Golf became a much bigger part of my life during these years in Manila. I assembled my first set of clubs, played many of the country's best courses, and held complimentary memberships at all the military ones. Each month the Fil-Am Golf Association organized a Friday outing. It'd begin mid-morning and run well into the night, requiring designated drivers to eventually get home.

Subic Bay Naval Base ultimately reverted to Philippine ownership and I found myself leading the closure of Cubi Point airfield. I transferred much of the associated equipment to the Philippine military. On the day of the official turnover ceremony, I flew Ambassador John Negroponte and his wife to Subic Bay, and in the process made the last landing on Cubi Point while it remained a U.S. possession. It seemed ironic that the U.S. Navy's pearl-of-the-Orient airfield allowed its final landing to be executed by an Air Force pilot with an Army co-pilot.

I met a girl during this time frame who soon became a big part of my life. I'd moved into a small but very comfortable apartment on the Seafront Compound. At the time, I had a dog and a cat and I didn't have anyone to keep an eye on them when off flying overnight trips. A girl nicknamed Bot agreed to keep an eye on things and we almost immediately bonded as a two-person team for life. She managed all things in the apartment and started accompanying me to Angeles City on the weekends. She loved flying, and of course, I couldn't resist such an attitude. But, why Angeles City …

Angelica and Bot join me on our scooter.

Chapter 34

Let's get one thing straight. There's a big difference between a pilot and an aviator. One is a technician; the other is an artist in love with flight.
– Unknown.

ONE OF OUR U.S. EMBASSY AIRCRAFT mechanics introduced me to a grass-roots start-up flying operation near Angeles City. A British businessman from Taiwan by the name of Gordon Boyce bought an entire ultra-light and sport plane flying club, packed it into forty-foot containers, and shipped it to the Philippines. He already owned a deteriorated hotel and wanted to pair it with flight training. I spent most weekends with two fellow flyers, Bill Wright and Fred Griffin, helping assemble the clubhouse and aircraft. Our small group fashioned a pair of very short runways and began test-flying what we'd assembled. My initial checkout consisted of one pattern followed by a second to confirm the first landing hadn't been a fluke. We taxied to the clubhouse where Bill unstrapped and gave his seat to an Air Transportation Office safety officer. We flew the short hop to Clark Airfield where I landed on the cleared tarmac area directly in front of the tower. The original runways remained unusable, buried under a foot of ash. This gave me the distinction of being the first Air Force officer to land an aircraft on Clark Airfield since the 1991 volcano.

The Angeles City Flying Club began operations out of Mabiga, a small community north of Angeles City. We signed a deal to fly action segments in the 1994 Philippine movie Geron Olivar. It starred the Governor of Pampanga, Lito Lapid, Actor of the Year, Edu Manzano, and a seventeen-year-old heart-throb by the name of Jackie Forster. Filming would soon begin at Cubi Point.

Bot climbed into the tiny sports plane behind me, cinched her seatbelt, and hung on tight as we launched from Mabiga's tiny grass strip. We passed the Santa Rita gap forty-five minutes later and watched in awe as Cubi Point's natural beauty unfolded a thousand feet below us. We felt like birds soaring in the sky, untethered and feeling the breeze.

Bot and I became good friends with Edu Manzano, an ex-Air Force airman who'd returned from the U.S. to his homeland where he became a popular movie actor. He and the other stars always ate lunch on-site near the ocean. That's when I drove from our filming location to base operations and asked the young airmen to join me and meet the movie stars. It didn't take long before I became the most popular guy around. It struck me as odd that of our expat group, only Bot and I preferred mingling with the actors over rushing off to MacDonald's for hamburgers.

I took military leave during the week of filming and sealed my lips to anyone at work about the movie. This proved to be too much fun and I feared that somehow the Chief of JUSMAG-PHIL would find a reason why I shouldn't be involved. Mum's the word. It became a bit harder when I crash-landed an ultra-light along the beach. The engine had fouled and sputtered, getting progressively worse until quitting. The shoreline sported a thin ribbon of sand in front of a hundred-foot sheer cliff. That's where I landed … with a two-foot landing distance! From there, I climbed a steep path up the cliff, found a suitable ultra-light, and launched on another flight. A front-page article in the

Manila-based tabloid Abante Tonite embellished the whole episode. Fortunately, the Embassy didn't notice.

It'd been twenty-three years since I enlisted in the Air Force, and I considered that longevity to be award-worthy. The decision to retire came easily, however. A hundred new opportunities awaited. I just had to find them. Gordon offered me a job managing the Angeles City Flying Club and I accepted. In so many ways, it seemed a foolish choice, but ironically, it turned out to be one of the best choices I ever made. Adventure opened its arms and once again we embraced. This foretold a different kind of fun.

Gordon didn't pay much but the benefits pretty much made up for it. He purchased several abandoned houses in the well-established Carmenville Subdivision and let Bot and I live in one he'd recently renovated – rent-free. Talk about a huge upgrade from the unfurnished, thirty-five dollars per month apartment we'd been occupying on weekends. There'd be no more parking the scooter in its single room, no more sleeping on a flimsy mattress on the floor, no more so many things. Food and drinks from his hotel bounced between cheap and free. I settled into a routine of supervising aircraft maintenance, airfield construction, and instructing seemingly suicidal Korean and Chinese student pilots. Over time, I became the conduit for resolving Air Transportation Office issues. My past U.S. Embassy association brought with it unexpected stature from Philippine administrators. I wrote a 150-page manual on Philippine sport-plane operations, including a multitude of definitions, safety guidelines, and certification standards. It became the basis for future Philippine Sport Plane Air

Directives. The Assistant Secretary of the Air Transportation Office, Panfilo V. Villaruel, Jr., the equivalent of our FAA Director, became a respected friend.

Most days came and went as expected – morning flight instruction, lunch, afternoon flight instruction, dinner, a few drinks, and then repeat the cycle. Occasionally a few bolts of adrenaline shocked my system when the Grim Reaper came within arm's reach.

We eventually flight-tested twenty dissimilar aircraft and made them available for lessons. Maintenance records didn't exist up to this point, so we modified inspection timing and critical part replacement cycles. But the lack of historical record-keeping made flying these things risky.

One day while in the traffic pattern at two hundred feet, the sport plane's engine suddenly fouled and quit. Easy-peasy. I turned toward the infield, maintained fifty miles per hour, and landed like a seasoned pro. Our longest runway stretched its grassy surface almost four hundred feet until terminating at a wire fence.

Several Quicksilver MXL-2 Sports served as our primary training aircraft.

Several months later I found myself a bit higher over our postage-stamp airfield in a Quick-Silver ultralight when aileron and elevator control stopped working. Stick full left… nothing. Stick full right… again, nothing. Power to idle, airspeed just above stall, meaning slow. The frail aircraft descended slowly but vertically and landed with a few feet to spare.

Another day I flew a nervous student on his first flight. We no sooner turned crosswind (that first turn after getting airborne and gaining some altitude) than the engine simply quit. I aimed for a narrow dirt path ahead. It'd be our target, but first I had to clear a telephone line. We slowed trying to glide over the wire, then slowed some more. We'd get tangled in the wire if I didn't take immediate action! Oh oh … nose full down. I dove straight toward the ground to gain whatever airspeed I could. Then prayed I had enough of it to flare without driving everything underground. The student appeared terrified at this point and the landing seemed a bit firm. I think we bent a few support tubes but made it! Almost. The path I'd landed on crossed a dirt road with concrete tabs to mark its borders. The nosewheel struck one of the tabs and caused the ultralight to cartwheel once or twice. A huge cloud of dust enveloped our upright tangle of fabric and guide wires.

A thought flashed through my head.

I just died.

I existed in a featureless sandy opaque cloud. I didn't hurt. There didn't appear to be any blood splattered about … and then I realized that dirt engulfed me and not heaven. That flight ended the student's desire to fly. I returned to the air an hour later.

This Russian Aviatika crashed fifteen minutes after I flew it for the last time.

Others crashed too. Twice, a propeller disintegrated after having been torqued too tightly to the hub. Another club member landed in a rice paddy after his engine fouled. He could have and should have continued the very short distance to the airfield, but elected to land immediately. When the aircraft touched down in the watery rice furrows it flipped forward, pressing the pilot into the muck. He almost drowned before freeing himself.

The Chief 747 Evaluator Pilot for Philippine Airlines, Capt Jim Piamonte, showed up one day with a borrowed Russian Aviatika-MAI-890 ultralight biplane.

Despite its heavy-duty Russian tank-like construction, it outperformed anything we currently flew. Forget about keeping the ball centered. Its tail sashayed left and right so much it felt like riding a mechanical bull. This little power ball ended up being a blast to fly.

On the day of the Aviatika's demise, I'd flown and almost crashed it myself. Banking sixty degrees while seventy-five feet above the overrun is a dangerous landing maneuver, and worse, I lost all control authority. I couldn't level the wings or pull up and would crash if I didn't. I chose full power, which may seem counter-intuitive, but it worked. Next, Bill Wright flew several patterns. Then Jim took off.

The engine failed at 150 feet as he turned left. Airspeed evaporated. The wings stalled and he quickly rolled inverted as the nose pointed directly toward the ground. He crashed before our eyes! Several of us instinctively rushed toward the sugarcane field.

Halfway there a cold shiver grabbed my heart.

I hope he isn't all blood and guts.

I found Jim in one piece although his shoes had forcibly shot off his feet. His left ankle twisted unnaturally sideways. My stomach soured. We pulled him from the aircraft as gently as possible and laid him on top of two twelve-foot wooden slats that had been hastily pulled from the top of a shipping crate. Those long slats caused the rear ambulance doors to remain open after we loaded him in its back. At the hospital, a janitor sawed off two feet of the planks so he'd fit in the elevator taking him for x-rays. Jim survived and eventually recovered. My endearment to the Air Transportation Office increased significantly after I submitted an investigative accident report where I'd correctly identified the cause of the crash but laid out the evidence in such a way that it absolved the pilot – a rare instance of political correctness.

Shortly thereafter, Assistant Secretary Villaruel asked me to act as his Philippines Safety Officer for sports plane and ultralight operations. I focused on the Angeles City Flying Club and kept our bacon out of the frying pan as best I could. Then, rumors of unusual flying habits on the resort island of Borocay surfaced. Our first maintenance technician had been hired to support the island's two sport planes and one of our weaker students became the chief pilot. On his first attempted flight, after we certified him as a pilot, he taxied into a concrete wall while talking to his passenger wife. He prided himself on flying at or below a hundred feet for most of every flight. He struck me as a disaster waiting to happen.

I drove to Manila and popped into Secretary Villaruel's office. He'd sent an ATO safety engineer to inspect the operation two weeks earlier and received a good report. However, it didn't address several significant issues. This situation occasionally happens after businessmen provide an under-the-table gratuity. Those inspections represented good times for the evaluator if he properly pre-announced his arrival. Everything would be readied for his cursory review, an expensive room at a nice hotel would be reserved, and everyone would be happy.

"I suggest you send someone undercover to observe operations first-hand and please don't pre-announce the inspection."

"Why?" Villaruel asked.

"Because you have an issue there and you don't know it. I think there's a good chance you'll see an ultralight accident before long…"

Two weeks later, the pilot killed himself and an innocent passenger when they flew into a palm tree.

Chapter 35

Sometimes, flying feels too godlike to be attained by man. Sometimes, the world from above seems too beautiful, too wonderful, too distant for human eyes to see.
– Charles A. Lindbergh

MaxAir Drifters, powered by 50hp Rotax engines. Only a couple of us had formation training but that didn't keep the others from getting close.

ORIENTATION FLIGHTS BECAME THE highlight of every day. More often than not we'd head toward the two-hundred-foot-deep canyons that the Sacobia River carved into the ash flows. I always flew from the backseat because, in addition to being more challenging, it left the passenger feeling like a bird in the unobstructed open air. The canyon's width felt extremely narrow and demanded full attention and quick reactions. The thrill factor topped the charts and left memories for a lifetime.

When not in the canyons, we flew tight overlapping wing-tip formation. Persistent memories of my struggles with air-to-air refueling no longer held the same intensity. I mastered the art of getting close.

The flying club participated in major Angeles City festivities. We flew orientation rides from the old 13th Air Force parade grounds and circled gigantic hot air balloons during Pampanga's annual Hot Air Balloon Festival.

One day a local pastor wandered into the clubhouse and asked if I'd scatter paper flyers announcing an upcoming church festival and he'd pay for the service.

Why not?

An ill-advised leaflet drop from this Rans S-12 scared the bejesus out of me.

A better answer slapped me in the face shortly thereafter. I climbed into the first available aircraft, a Rans S-12 Coyote, and strapped the box of flyers onto the adjoining seat. Ten minutes later I found myself a hundred feet above his church and surrounding barrio. That's when "Why not?" changed to "Hell no!"

Every time I took my hand off the throttle to grab some flyers, the engine power abruptly reduced to idle. That hand needed to stay in place. To make this work, I'd have to squeeze my knees together and hold the control stick between my legs. I held it steady while reaching with my right hand for the pamphlets. Seemed easy enough as long as I didn't nose over and crash. I grabbed a large handful of flyers and threw them out and down … oops!

The airflow sucked the flyers back into the cockpit, everywhere, but mostly plastered across the windscreen. Pamphlets completely obstructed my forward view. I climbed. Once again, that sour feeling in my stomach returned. I grabbed a few of the easy-to-reach flyers and stuffed them in my pockets. The ones on the windscreen would require dexterity and more importantly, luck to remove. I unstrapped the shoulder harness, half stood, squeezed the stick between my knees, and as quickly as possible stretched forward and grabbed a couple of flyers.

The aircraft abruptly nosed down. The throttle crawled back to idle. Sit down! Get control. Stuff flyers under my shirt. Repeat.

What the hell? Don't ever do this again!

I instructed young Filipinos, crazy Koreans, a Japanese gentleman who always wore white gloves, and an assortment of others. Two young German party animals drank beer with their morning eggs and found themselves grounded until learning the bottle-to-throttle rules. Communications played a big role in keeping the business afloat. Student pilots, no matter how good or bad, learned more quickly from a calm knowledgeable instructor. An insulted foreign student would leave for the day never to be seen again. I learned to be tough with a friendly tone and explained the "why" behind the rules. Dangerous pilots who refused to understand flying discipline soon found the exit. The rest kept coming back.

On occasion, curious hawks soared alongside us. It balanced the daily stress.

A fast-talking expat named Dave managed Gordon's hotel, the Woodland Park Resort … until Philippine Immigration officials placed a target on his back. A pedophile without a visa represented easy prey for a corrupt Immigration official. Dave fled to Thailand. He'd later return only to be stabbed to death, twenty-seven times, by the father of an underage victim. Gordon asked me to assume management of the hotel in addition to the flying club.

Woodland Park Resort flashed potential but had been neglected into a state of disrepair. To find its non-descript entrance one had to venture down an isolated dirt road and walk through a poorly-lit vehicle-repair yard. The reception desk could be found farther into a poorly lit area. After dark, the walk could be downright dangerous.

Fourteen-year-old girls, who Dave referred to as vampires, wandered from room to room in the evenings. The hotel's mixed occupancy consisted of short-time customers, Dave's fellow pedophiles, and a smattering of relatively normal tourists. I viewed the place as a low-cost dump with a large swimming pool, but one that held profit potential. Major redirection and a bit of forward vision started the journey to respectability.

On day one, I instructed the guards to keep the vampires out. They'd no longer be allowed on the premises, effective immediately. Affected guests confronted me and I suggested they move elsewhere. The riff-raff disappeared.

Philippine labor law established existing pay standards.

"Are we paying minimum wage?" I asked.

No one could answer the question. I dug through government publications and realized we paid below the minimum, but not by much. The Philippine Department of Labor set the minimum wage based on industry and location. I adjusted Woodland Park Resort's daily pay upward by a few pesos, adjusted for night differential, holidays, and a myriad of other pay nuances. I also withheld Social Security and Income Taxes. To calculate all this, I wrote a computer program and provided pay stubs.

Another Philippine labor quirk categorized employees with less than six months tenure as "probationary." These employees could be terminated without cause, and more importantly, without legal recourse. Employees on the payroll longer than six months became much more difficult to terminate without legal repercussions. We retained employees as long as they performed well and spent a lot of time in court if we fired them. It became a happy, friendly, and loyal workforce.

The hotel consisted of thirty rooms and a beautiful swimming pool. Everything else needed work. I envisioned family-oriented landscaping that tied the natural beauty of the property to upgraded facilities. The open-air restaurant and palm-shaded grounds would appeal to wedding parties and family outings. We enhanced open areas with decorative bushes, displayed exotic birds in large enclosures, and planted a lot of colorful flowers. But first, we addressed the lack of perimeter security and the poorly located entrance.

A new security wall neared completion a month later. All the commotion caused some unintended consequences, however, like slimy-skinned two-foot-long lizards approaching tables in the open-air restaurant. Bot and I stirred up a pair of Philippine cobras one evening while inspecting the wall. Late one afternoon, I noticed ten employees lugging a  stretched-out ten-foot-long python toward the restaurant. They'd pulled it from under a bamboo clump. We gave it to a Canadian guest whose Filipina girlfriend barbequed it two days later.

The new entrance took some planning. I organized a fifteen-man workforce to carve a narrow roadway from the far front corner of the property to the interior. Three workers cemented thousands of rocks along a terraced roadside wall while the rest of us mixed, poured, and smoothed a concrete entry road. We employed an old three-bag mechanical mixer that sped up the process considerably. Twelve-hour days tended to end with the consumption of a case of San Miguel beer. As long as I worked alongside the others, production speed sizzled.

Unfortunately, the stretch of road from the new entrance to MacArthur Highway remained badly pot-holed. The Barangay Captain liked the idea of my workers paving his road for free and the City Engineers concurred … as long as we bought the concrete and did the work. What the heck? We agreed and I organized the workers. Before long, we enjoyed much-improved hotel access.

With so many of the major projects now completed, more interesting projects warranted consideration ... like leading treks up Mt. Pinatubo. Every Tuesday at 9:30 a.m., I provisioned a group of trekkers with water and fruit and then drove them through towering elephant grass to a remote Negrito village. We hiked along river beds from there, climbed up and down sheer cliffs, crossed a wide area of quicksand, and eventually entered a deep narrow gap in the mountains. Streams that'd been cold now became tepid, and higher up the mountain water flowed steamy-hot. Each trek covered a little over ten miles and in a word, the tourists felt exhausted afterward.

I organized a bachelor's party every so often ... sort of The Hangover Parts I, II, and III combined. It usually kicked off at sunset with pitchers of cheap but tasty margaritas. As the designated driver and party guide, I loaded everyone into the back of the hotel's Toyota Tamaraw. I'd paid each of the ten bars on our itinerary in advance and the routine repeated itself at each stop. Girls provided glasses of rum and coke, and bottles of San Miguel to everyone. A floor show seemed to always begin once the bachelor took a stage-side seat. Before leaving, an assistant party guide hired a working girl to accompany the bachelor until we finished visiting all the remaining bars. I ultimately returned the revelers to the hotel pool for more drinks and food. At that point, I got on my scooter and headed home.

The morning after held little pain for me, but for most others, it verged on a medical emergency. Cool 6 a.m. air, steaming coffee, and morning newspapers ... invigorating.

The hotel property had been titled to Gordon's girlfriend, Reza. She turned out to be a delightful young woman, but her father, brother, and sisters came with a condescending air of superiority. The brother had recently earned a degree in architecture and Gordon enlisted his services to design an additional thirty rooms. He placed the entrances on the wrong side of the building and designed them so small that bed frames couldn't be moved into the rooms. His redesign didn't look much better.

One day, Gordon asked me to gainfully employ the sister as she wanted to learn hotel and restaurant management. Within the first hour, she demanded I initiate a complete financial audit. I sent her home. It became instantly clear that my time in the Philippines had neared its end.

Chapter 36

Simple solutions seldom are…
– Alfred North Whitehead

DAD PLAYED TENNIS ONCE A WEEK WITH A long-time friend named Joe LaForce. Joe had built our house on 1221 Oregon Street back in the 1950s and now owned a niche business creating commercial door frames. He'd been looking for a solution to translate his outdated computer program software to IBM's non-compatible RPG-IV programming language.

He currently paid a contractor to rewrite the code for all of his financial applications because it seemed marginally cheaper than buying entirely new off-the-shelf software. His specialized programmer had written a partially effective conversion program.

Whatever data didn't convert properly required reprogramming the old process with new code. The programmer also wanted to start a separate business running his conversion process for others. Joe wanted an independent party to evaluate his options, including an abbreviated business plan for the "new business" option.

During one of those weekly tennis matches, Dad seized the opportunity to mention my recent return from the Philippines. Before I knew it, I found myself face-to-face with Joe LaForce and John McMullen, the company president. They hired me to complete the desired analysis. I took a big breath and mentally organized a plan.

Jeff McGlachlin, the head of IT, tutored me on RPG-IV and conveyed the gist of its architecture and limitations. My evaluation would answer two questions: would LaForce find it more cost-effective to convert software or buy an off-the-shelf suite? Would financing a software conversion start-up business prove to be financially prudent? I researched everything for several weeks, crunched through the numbers, and wrote the report. I feared that after Joe read it, he'd politely send me packing.

In a nutshell, I suggested that converting and reprogramming existing computer code came with a high cost, introduced unnecessary risk, and would result in one-of-a-kind software. Reliably updating this stuff didn't offer an easy path to the future.

LaForce could buy off-the-shelf software now or they could buy it in the future … in other words, pay the piper now and be done with it, or pay programmer fees now and pay the piper later. I recommended buying off-the-shelf software rather than converting.

LaForce's core business included manufacturing doorframes and supplying specialty goods such as fire extinguisher cabinets, bathroom stalls, etc. Developing software programs requires a vastly different skill set. I explained that starting a software conversion company represented risk with diminishing returns over time. I sensed they wanted me to manage the software conversion business and I politely suggested they count me out.

After several days of deliberation, Joe asked if I could create a product catalog, and at the same time formalize his Marketing Department. His request caught me off guard. The Air Force taught me that I could do darned near anything. I responded that I could, and that's how a most unusual couple of years began.

Bot and I bought a farmhouse with a four-stall pole building out back. It would store my homebuilt Q-2 aircraft and a highly customized Porsche 911 that I'd imported from Germany. Our small family delightfully isolated ourselves from the commotion of Green Bay. We found ourselves surrounded by cornfields where rustling sounds whispered, "Come in and explore a bit." Apples hung low from our trees and farmland neighbors opened their hearts to us.

LaForce's non-existent product catalog had been a ten-year project that never gained traction. I wondered why on earth it'd been so hard to create.

I needed page layout and photo processing software so I purchased Quark Express and Photoshop and undertook the tedious process of learning how to use them. I scheduled interviews with each department head in an attempt to gain an understanding of how to present specific hardware. I decided to start with something easy ... door hinges.

How hard can it be to sell a door hinge?

What size door? Three hinges or four? How heavy? Wooden residential or lead-lined for a hospital's x-ray department? Will it need bearings? Will it extend out from the edge? Envision a boomerang-shaped hinge. What material? Bronze, steel, copper, etc. With so many options, it seemed an impossible challenge to fit it on a single page. Organization would be the key. I took baby steps with a hinge chapter that opened with a general discussion of all the considerations and followed that with a step-by-step process to arrive at the desired hinge. Door knobs, door closers, kick pads, bumper stops, and on and on – one step at a time.

Nine months later I presented the company with a 225-page catalog that ultimately became the industry standard. Well, sort of. To my knowledge, it represented the only comprehensive product catalog for doors, frames, and construction specialties. By default, it also became the standard.

Our little marketing department created the company's first webpage, attended tradeshows, advertised in phonebooks and newspapers, and generally kept busy. Our favorite time of the year, however, occurred during the deer-hunting season when the Green Bay Packers football team captivated everyone's attention.

I controlled nineteen season tickets and provided them on a game-by-game basis to our best customers. Hosting pre-game tailgate parties soon became another major undertaking. One year, we leased several mobile homes and reserved two stadium parking spots. We'd use only one mobile home and then only because of its bathroom and filled the other space with food, drinks, and people. We borrowed a marching band for one game.

Originally, the company hosted post-game tailgate parties. Guests consumed one last drink for the road while the stadium parking lot emptied around them. When I pointed out the dangers of drinking until the beer ran out and then driving home, and also noted the obvious liability issues should there be an accident, the post-game parties became ad hoc rather than company-sponsored.

As patrons left the pre-game tailgate party for the game, I packed everything into a large LaForce panel truck and drove across town to return chafing dishes, tables, and booze. A painful stress headache always developed by the time I got home and it immobilized me until the next morning.

Several of us joined the Wednesday Noon Optimist Club. Membership consisted mostly of older businessmen from town but also included several successful women. Their varied perspectives on any number of topical issues moderated my views, and more importantly, opened my eyes to viewing a single issue in a variety of ways. It reinforced the idea of not getting too set in my opinions until I'd heard both sides of an issue.

On non-Optimist Wednesdays, I embarked on exploratory runs around the west side of Green Bay. One day I investigated the city's power plant, another day I wove through an old residential section. One winter, I discovered a great four-miler to and from Lambeau Field football stadium. Unshoveled sidewalks presented both a footing challenge and a keep-my-shoes-dry challenge. Bitter cold air seemed strangely appropriate when the stadium came into view.

I realized over time that all the corporate officers appeared to be my age or younger. Their youthful fresh approach to work permeated the offices. I loved working there and considered the corporate officers to be rock solid. That vitality would carry the company well into the future. However, it offered little promotion potential. As the company expanded, I grew restless.

I received an email from Skippy Carson who at the time worked as an Air Force contractor. He announced global job opportunities for Air Force mission planners, an area in which all the addressees shared expertise. My curiosity piqued. According to Skippy, there'd be a job for everyone. I submitted a resume.

I kept thinking about my job at LaForce. It offered lifelong security, presented emerging challenges in an expanding market, and included a very strong and easy-to-work-with corporate office. Plus, I also planned and ran corporate tailgate parties at Lambeau Field for Green Bay Packers football games. It couldn't get much better ... but rubbing shoulders with military flyers, managing their cutting-edge software, and more directly defending our Nation's freedoms ran deep in my veins. A Lockheed Martin manager called ...

The following week I flew to Nashua, New Hampshire, rented a car, and drove to Merrimack for the night. The next morning, I found Sanders, a Lockheed Martin Company corporate office, and interviewed. Three of us underwent the initial screening, and I ended up being offered a position on their new contract. I became the first hire on a global contract that continues to this day after more than twenty-one years.

I returned to another Sanders office in Merrimack two weeks later and assisted with the program startup. Tom Lachance assumed the Program Manager position and transferred from Lockheed Martin Technical Operations when he accepted the job. Clayton Wong, another early hire, along with Susan Guerrero from Colorado and several others from around the country joined the team. We worked for a month hiring and processing approximately eighty other system support technicians.

Before anyone could travel to their assigned units, security clearances needed to be obtained and coordinated. Letters of Authorization, which looked quite similar to military orders, spelled out the details of each assignment. It became a handful to process everything. Travel approvals happened quickly at some bases and very slowly at others. I'd be the Asian Regional Manager located at Yokota Air Base in Tokyo, Japan.

Another prerequisite included certification as a Linux system administrator and hands-on familiarity with the twenty-four containers that housed the mission-planning equipment. Linux certification training turned out to be brutal. Classroom lectures and lab sessions spanned ten to twelve hours each day for two weeks. We struggled to complete lengthy reading assignments at night before stealing a couple of hours of sleep. Like running a marathon, it took a lot of mental and physical endurance.

I boarded a flight bound for Tokyo in December 1999. Bot and our daughter, Angelica, remained in Wisconsin until I found an apartment and got settled. Tokyo's Narita Airport featured an expansive terminal filled with high-end international retail stores, food stalls under large Chinese and Japanese characters, and most of all, foreign passengers. On the one hand, it felt warm and inviting while on the other, it represented an entry into a new and mysterious culture. Fortunately, I'd researched travel from Narita Airport to Yokota Air Base. If I could find the Yokota-bound bus in a sea of similar buses, I'd be home free. It took a bit of looking, but I found it.

The bus ride lasted two eye-popping hours through the heart of nighttime Tokyo. Wide canals and river-like waterways shared space with its nine million residents. Rainbow Bridge crossed Tokyo Bay 150 feet above the water but felt more like a glimpse of low earth orbit. Nerves tightened as we headed up toward its crest. I prayed there wouldn't be an earthquake. Then the bright-orange structure of Tokyo Tower passed to our right. Elevated two-lane roadways swerved left and right between incredibly high office buildings. Corporate logos clung to the higher stories or perched atop slightly lower rooftops. I looked down three or four levels below us and gawked at ground-level sidewalks filled with pedestrians. Train tracks four and five across ran parallel to our bus before curving right or left and disappearing into a sea of buildings. Some dipped underground and disappeared. Deeper down, subway tunnels snaked their way beneath Tokyo's glossy skyscrapers. I tried memorizing the route we followed but lost concentration. The feeling of being adrift at sea or maybe stranded in an enchanted world tickled my mind. It felt intimidating and exciting at the same time.

The familiar smell of JP-8 aviation fuel welcomed me to Yokota's flight line. The aroma comforted my soul and conveyed a warmth felt when returning home from a long absence. My arrival came as a surprise to the 374th Airlift Wing. The contracting office had no idea that I'd be working on their base, and I hoped the others who would move to northern Japan, Okinawa, and Korea would experience a better reception. My new office consisted of a desk and computer in an archaic building once occupied by a Japanese kamikaze squadron. I networked a dozen mission-planning laptop computers within the first two weeks and developed a process for updating the myriad of data they required.

A contracted Japanese cleaning lady caught our attention when she habitually looked at paper scraps before throwing them into her trash bag. We soon left only meaningless notes in the trash and shredded everything else or loaded it into a burn bag. It seemed a bit strange but we didn't give it further thought.

At some point, we noticed her absence and found out that her employment had been terminated when the Office of Special Investigations discovered her husband to be a North Korean.

Bot periodically experienced significant issues with the medications she took. When I mentioned this to Tom Lachance, he offered me a position as his Deputy Program Manager. He convinced me that the move would return us to more familiar medical care if it should be needed. Leaving Japan would be tough, but we decided to move. We packed our bags and boarded a plane for Colorado Springs.

Chapter 37

Nothing is really work unless you would rather be doing something else.
– J.M. Farrie

WE RETURNED TO THE UNITED STATES FOR what we thought would be a permanent stay. As it turned out, our new residence only lasted a couple of years.

Lockheed Martin Technical Operations occupied a reflective blue-tinted-glass five-story building near the Colorado Springs airport. Its prominent location in the business park convinced me I'd become a heavy hitter. I slid my security badge across the card reader and the doors of program management opened before me.

An endless list of issues included weird personnel situations I never imagined could exist. Officially I managed 250-plus support technicians and unofficially also handled any number of issues from two other international programs.

One representative insisted the military required him to work sixteen hours a day to support twenty-four-hour operations. The contract covered only half that time. His military boss called.

"Where is this guy?"

We realized something didn't add up. We had no way of knowing he left his work location if he didn't tell us. As it turned out, he hopped on a military flight to Germany for a mini-vacation. We put him on a more permanent one shortly thereafter.

Another representative couldn't afford the "key money" to lease a decent South Korean apartment. He and his family lived in a tiny unit with a crack in the wall so wide that snow blew through it on stormy nights. We worked a bit of financial magic and got him into a better place.

Then September 11th happened. Work stalled for several weeks before accelerating into overdrive. Contingency plans took shape. I mailed visa applications to Turkmenistan, Uzbekistan, and Tajikistan embassies in Washington D.C. When two technicians refused to fly home from training in Salt Lake City, we directed them to rent cars and drive home. One drove to Idaho and the other to the east coast. My wife laughed at their fears.

"… you should tell them they can't drive to Afghanistan."

Two days later while jogging, I detoured into the Colorado Springs Police Department helicopter hangar and volunteered my services. As luck would have it, they'd been looking for tactical control officers to fly alongside their pilots. This job linked the helicopter with ground control stations. There'd be a month-long training period after which I'd begin flying late-night missions.

I shadowed a young officer as he apprehended an armed crook while he tried to cash a stolen check. Another night, I patrolled seedy minority bars with a tough female officer. She appeared confident and calm. My nerves went to full alert as I learned about connecting with young adults in deteriorating neighborhoods. Respect gained during peaceful times bridged the communication gap when drugs and alcohol became factors. And then … the flying began.

Locals called us the Ghetto Copter guys. Air Unit 1 consisted of a handful of officer pilots and a single maintenance technician. One pilot of Iranian descent had been a U.S. Marine Cobra pilot. Jim had been a U.S. Army aviator and training officer, and Jeff had learned to fly helicopters on his own dime. Each represented a unique background and each performed exceptionally well. I loved flying with these guys. Before long, I shared stick time and logged many hours in each of the unit's two Bell Jet Rangers.

The pilots found themselves limited to twelve-hour workdays when flying. As a volunteer tactical officer, I seemed exempt from that rule and never asked the question. I typically flew on Friday and Saturday nights although I'd fly mid-week when asked. Fridays became ball-busters. I'd ride my Yamaha Road Star motorcycle to work at 6:30 a.m., change into a suit and tie, and work a normal day until 5 p.m. Then I'd change again and ride to the police hangar where I'd fly until 1:00 a.m. Every night something unusual made air patrolling memorable.

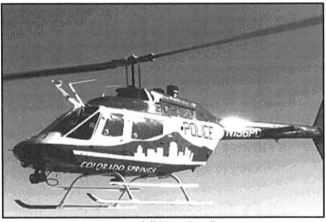

Colorado Springs Police Department's "Ghetto Copter"

One night a three-hundred-pound bull broke loose from its Pike's Peak or Bust Rodeo pen and headed northwest toward Manitou Springs. Our mission, find the rambunctious bull and track it until rodeo cowboys could either rope it or tranquilize it. We never did see the bull, but we did get lased over Manitou Springs. We descended without looking directly into the laser beam until a hundred feet over the suspect house. Squad cars arrived shortly thereafter and the lasing problem disappeared.

I arrived early one Saturday afternoon to find a pilot scrambling toward a helicopter. I jumped in next to him and got briefed on a high-speed chase taking place along Interstate 25 north of Pueblo. We planned to intercept the vehicle before it got to Colorado Springs, nosed over, and accelerated to 120 knots on an intercept course. Shortly before the intercept point, the suspect swerved through a highway underpass and disappeared into the desert. At least six patrol cars kicked up a cloud of brown dust as they pursued … we looked far and wide but couldn't spot the suspect's car. Sunset would arrive in forty-five minutes so finding it needed to happen quickly. We came across a mobile home with several cars parked, almost hidden, behind a secondary structure. It looked suspicious. We hovered fifty feet from the house and then circled to the vehicles. One of the license numbers matched. Then I received a call from the Pueblo Control Center stating that another resident in the area reported seeing a suspicious individual hiding behind a large cactus. We zipped over to that area. The suspect walked out from hiding and stood before our helicopter with hands raised over his head. Officers arrested him shortly thereafter.

On slower nights, I hover-taxied along the municipal airport's outer boundary and aimed our spotlight at the fence line to verify its security. The Jet Ranger flew like a leaf in the wind. It felt lightweight and could be a handful to control on gusty nights. We refueled mid-mission with the main rotor still turning. Cold winter air turned frigid under the rotor wash. Refueling didn't take long but it came with a bitter cold that penetrated my bones.

Toward the end of the first year in Colorado Springs, the Mission Planning Support Contract came up for a competitive rebid. As is the case with many government contracts, the winner would of necessity be a small business, preferably with a disabled minority female owner from Alaska. Lockheed Martin Technical Operations did not qualify, and unfortunately, we partnered with a losing small business. It felt more than a bit uncomfortable watching a crusty old retired Air Force General ramble on while briefing our proposal.

I wondered how that guy became a General. He'd lost the ability to actually do staff work and employ effective briefing skills.

I no longer had a major program to manage and found myself writing and managing contract proposals. I drove ninety minutes each morning to a Lockheed Martin proposal center outside Denver where I worked long hours before returning home. Worse, I filled an overhead position. In other words, the company compensated my work from a cost-of-doing-business account rather than from a specific contract position. I found that I preferred being associated with a contract and actually generating the flow of funds into the company.

That worry soon resolved itself when the Transportation Security Administration came into being. I asked to be loaned to Lockheed Martin Mission Systems where I'd lead a team designing security checkpoints throughout Nebraska and Colorado. My first major design effort commenced at Nebraska's Grand Island Airport.

As luck would have it on the day before leaving, I accidentally cut off a bit of my right index finger in a table saw mishap. I wrapped it in a washcloth and drove to the nearest Walgreens Pharmacy. It hurt and it throbbed, but it didn't disrupt the airport planning.

Our team returned to survey the Colorado Springs Airport and eventually completed all assigned tasks. We awaited equipment delivery and installation. Delay after delay wasted valuable time and I became more and more restless being officially non-productive, so I coordinated a comprehensive logistics and training plan for newly hired TSA security screeners. I convinced the airport director to provide us with an office and storage space. After creating and coordinating security badges, I developed training schedules, and so forth. Eventually, our airport design team disbanded, and I convinced the inbound Airport Security Director to hire me as his Assistant Federal Security Director for Screening, a GS-15 level position. The transition happened seamlessly except for ordering new business cards. I already knew the entire 170-person security team on a first-name basis and had written their training plans.

During the years that followed, I developed effective personnel staffing models and successfully defended them against an onslaught of seemingly arbitrary cuts. The many hours spent discussing work assumptions and resolving misunderstandings with TSA's personnel analyst minimized staffing reductions while optimizing a more realistic workforce.

I counseled and ultimately fired more screeners and managers than I ever imagined. The government's labor protection laws impressed me as being complex but fair, and I found inertia and burdensome regulations within the Department of Labor to be a major issue. OSHA and workplace disabilities offered legitimate worker protections, but when abused they became a manager's worst nightmare. Personnel management came with many important lessons. Evaluate performance, counsel, document, provide a path to success, evaluate again, repeat as necessary, and only then terminate.

Airport screening brought with it unique moments like when Olympic athletes came and went. Speed skater Apolo Anton Ohno regularly passed through the airport. We also experienced unusual screening challenges. The International Atomic Energy Agency team transited after inspecting the Pueblo Chemical Depot. We swabbed them and their equipment for evidence of lingering nuclear materials. International Defense Ministers held a conference in Colorado Springs and we dealt with their security teams. Fortunately, everyone handled their weapons appropriately. Interesting times…

The Transportation Security Administration secured not only our airports but also seaports and railways. The latter of these presented significant issues in that endless miles of rail seemed susceptible to compromise. My experience staffing crisis action cells in the region led to a national-level proposal for developing photographic displays with technical overlays and then sharing that data with regional and national crisis action staff. I found my efforts to be challenging and rewarding. But then an unexpected bump in the road took shape …

To secure U.S. citizenship for our second daughter, Marie, I needed to live with her for two years, overseas. Relinquishing the Assistant Federal Security Director position at Colorado Springs would otherwise have been unthinkable. While TSA staffed several overseas positions, the only opening covered airport security in Pakistan, Bangladesh, India, and Myanmar. I didn't care for the locations, and I also lacked the desired airport inspection experience for maintenance and food services. Fortunately, my old position at Yokota Air Base would soon be vacant and the thought of returning to Japan seemed a viable alternative. I resigned from TSA and packed my bags once again.

Chapter 38

When we rebuild a house, we are rebuilding a home. When we recover from disaster, we are rebuilding lives and livelihoods.
– Sri Mulyani Indrawati

NOVEMBER 2004. I RETURNED TO MY OLD position at Yokota Air Base in Tokyo, Japan. It felt odd replacing the very same computer technician who'd replaced me several years earlier. The closer I looked, the more troubled I became. Maybe the drop in performance resulted from a differing personality-driven approach or maybe it reflected simple professionalism. My cloistered predecessor became an unknown, spending large chunks of time hidden at his desk in a tiny storage closet. Neither aircrew nor commanders knew he existed. I verified it when I asked and asked, and asked some more. No one knew the guy. His computer became my computer and the reason for his isolated office clarified as gambling-related malware and adware popped up every few minutes – odd for a government machine. Good riddance.

Re-connecting with the aircrews started with moving into a real office, one without dividing walls or partitions. I needed human interaction, not privacy. Building a deployable aircraft mission planning capability came next. Before long, pilots and navigators knew me and asked software-related questions. Working closely with them fueled my sense of self-worth. These guys acted as professionals. I knew how they thought and what motivated their zest for flying. Meetings with the commanders provided a vision of how a proactive systems technician could improve their overall capability.

I lived alone in a rented house near the airbase. Bot and Angelica remained in Colorado Springs to finish the school year. Christmas in 2004 fell on a Saturday. I attended morning mass and loafed around the house most of the afternoon. The next morning, news of a nine-point-one-magnitude earthquake off the coast of Indonesia appeared on the Internet. It appeared to be a big one and as the day wore on, reports of devastation shocked the world.

The earthquake ruptured nine hundred miles of the ocean floor where the Indian and Australian tectonic plates converged. Over ten minutes, extended segments of the earth's crust pushed abruptly upward more than 130 feet. The result forced a gigantic, menacing tsunami. 230,000 lives would be lost within hours.

The city of Banda Aceh on the northern tip of Sumatra succumbed twenty minutes later. One-hundred-foot waves engulfed 100,000 men, women, and children, all of whom died instantly as the city disappeared underwater.

The tsunami surged in all directions at an incredible speed of five hundred miles per hour. Thailand, where vacationers littered the beach resorts of Phang Nga and Phuket, suffered next. Sunny skies and hot temperatures masked the approaching disaster. When shallow waters along the beach receded hundreds of yards into the ocean curiosity peaked. Minutes later a churning wall of water smashed inland, and 5,400 died.

Ten thousand people near the city of Chennai, India, drowned. More than thirty thousand people vanished under rising waters when the tsunami reached Sri Lanka.

A researcher from the National Oceanic and Atmospheric Administration Center for Tsunami Research reported -

> We took a boat all the way from the middle of Sumatra up to Banda Aceh, the hardest-hit area, and for hundreds of kilometers, it looked as if somebody had taken an eraser and erased everything underneath the twenty-meter line. The sheer scale of the destruction became mind-boggling.

At 9:30 p.m. a knock sounded on my door. Major Martinez, our Weapons and Tactics shop chief, and my operational boss stood in front of me.

"Can you get our computers updated tonight? We're most likely flying to Thailand in the morning. Can you deploy with us?"

My eyes blinked several times as I thought about what I'd just been asked. The computers wouldn't be a problem although it'd take more than a few hours to get them all organized. I'd need permission to fly on a C-130 to Thailand, both from my company and from the Air Force.

"Sure. I'll drive to base right away."

Thirty minutes later I entered keypad codes to access the mission planning rooms, then deactivated the motion sensors and confirmed entry with the security police. Packing all the computer components didn't present issues because I kept them prepped for just such an occurrence. The list of things to pack included laptops, printers, a router, switches, cables, power transformers, outlet adaptors, and so forth. Updating the data on each of the computers and then dry-running a tactical network took more time. The

National Geospatial-Intelligence Agency updated airspace, airport, and navigational aid data files every twenty-seven days. This data wouldn't have been loaded onto deployable laptops until shortly before departure. Normally, there'd be several weeks of advance notification. This situation developed much more quickly. There existed woefully little chart data for the Banda Aceh area – no low-level charts, no digitized terrain elevations, and no imagery. Google Earth didn't fully exist.

I sent an email to BAE Systems advising them I planned to deploy within a few hours and requested they approve my travel as soon as possible. On the Air Force side, I drafted a letter requesting Mission Essential Personnel status. That approval had been confirmed before departure.

At 4:30 a.m., I locked the mission planning room doors and headed home to pack. At 9:00 a.m. our C-130 departed on a three-hour flight to Okinawa, followed by an eight-hour flight to U-Taphao Royal Thai Naval Base, Thailand. I scrunched shoulder-to-shoulder between two king-sized maintainers. The webbed seating and a boxy hydraulic cart kept me from getting too comfortable. I read a Louis L'Amour novel.

The situation at U-Taphao remained fluid. We scattered four C-130s on the tarmac. The normally expansive and empty tarmac appeared jam-packed with a hundred former Soviet Union commercial airliners. The airport manager told us the Russian pilots had locked their aircraft and rode with the passengers to Pattaya or Jomtien. They'd be unreachable for the next two weeks when they'd return, refuel their aircraft, and depart.

The Air Force contracted with a U-Taphao-based company called Delta Golf for logistical support. DG maintained a small office with a wireless Internet router and it seemed to me that given the nature of the situation, they'd willingly share some of their bandwidth. My job included establishing an operations cell, and their office turned out to be the perfect place.

I'd gathered a fair amount of experience participating in disaster relief missions over the years. At the same time, a lot of things didn't seem obvious to commanders on their first such mission. This became especially true with aircrews. They wanted to start providing relief immediately, the sooner the better. But it seldom worked that way.

Aircraft became the delivery vehicles. USAID needed to preposition relief aid from its nearest global warehouses to a point where the aircraft could upload it. That often took days or weeks. When an aircraft arrived at the delivery destination, sufficient ground handling equipment such as forklifts needed to be available to offload it. Banda Aceh's airport had no such equipment.

It seemed obvious to the pilots that the Air Force should be directing operations. However, the primary service component for such operations had always been the Marine Corps because their operational scope extended far beyond the limited amount of relief provided via airlift. Long-term aid involved rebuilding infrastructure – roads, bridges, key facilities, and even local governments.

My unofficial job included advising the Air Force contingent commanders on mission tasking strategies vis-à-vis the Marine Task Force Commander.

On May 27, 2006, a 6.3 magnitude earthquake destroyed sixty thousand houses and killed more than six thousand people near the city of Yogyakarta in Central Java, Indonesia. U.S. government-to-government relations with Indonesia remained cool up to that point but warmed slowly. Providing humanitarian relief for this disaster provided another opportunity for the governments to engage in an area of mutual interest.

We deployed two C-130 cargo aircraft to Singapore several days later. I found myself once again cramped into a webbed seat with my feet draped over the wheels of a maintenance stand. It ended up being a long, tiring flight that terminated at Paya Labar Air Base. We boarded a bus and headed to a nice hotel in the heart of Singapore.

The next morning I cobbled together a mission planning network within the tight confines of a small room and hallway. We waited ...

USAID encountered issues moving relief supplies to Paya Labar and eventually moved them elsewhere. Ultimately, trucks carried the supplies to Yogyakarta. We packed our equipment and flew back to Tokyo.

April 2008. We call them hurricanes in the Atlantic, typhoons in the Pacific, and cyclones in the Indian Ocean and Oceania. Normally, cyclones held little interest for us because they occurred so far away. The countries most affected included India and Bangladesh, and of these, India appeared mostly self-sufficient in supporting their internal needs. Bangladesh, on the other hand, experienced severe flooding at least once every four to five years. Its 164 million citizens lived an impoverished life only feet above sea level.

Bangladesh shared its border with Burma, which suffered the ill effects of cyclones to a somewhat lesser extent.

Burma's topography varied drastically from the Himalayas in the north and the lower mountains farther south. However, the Irrawaddy Delta to the southwest of Yangon encompassed a low-lying region inhabited by thousands of poor farmers and fishermen.

Cyclone Nargis strengthened to a category four storm in the Bay of Bengal. We watched as 130mph winds made landfall and ultimately killed more than 138,350 people. Government-to-government relations with Burma had thawed somewhat, prompting a U.S. offer of disaster relief and humanitarian support. During the relief operations, the U.S. officially referred to Burma by its current moniker, Myanmar. Four aircraft repositioned to U-Taphao, Thailand, and airlifted supplies began flowing into Yangon.

I joined Major Kelly Holbert aboard Thai Airways and flew to Bangkok. From there we arranged for a private driver to transport us to Pattaya. We set up shop the next morning.

The relief operation became somewhat unique. Very limited information existed on flying into Yangon's airport or getting support once there. I directed our young intel airman to question the aircrew upon their return, to get a sense of the airfield condition and the availability of maintenance support should an aircraft have issues. His job of determining something as simple as airfield lighting and the availability of a power cart seemed beyond his reach. We always took enough fuel for the round-trip so refueling never became an issue.

He failed miserably on the first day. On the second day, he dragged himself into the office with hickies covering most of his neck. I got permission and transferred him to the far end of the tarmac where he'd support the Marines while planning their missions. He lasted four days before they sent him back.

Despite rumors of significant inefficiencies in distributing the relief aid we airlifted, we collectively felt good about having done our part. As with most air missions, it remained difficult to imagine the trauma experienced by those receiving it.

On March 11, 2011, Thailand's Cope Tiger military training exercise progressed smoothly through its first week. Over the weekend we received reports of a large earthquake north of Tokyo. Wives at Yokota Air Base messaged their husbands. An earthquake had shaken the area at a magnitude of 9.1 and the ensuing tsunami had devastated the coastline.

The extent of the disaster became clear by the following Monday, but not in a good way. The Japanese government feared that thousands of citizens had died after more than two hundred square miles of coastal land flooded under waves estimated to be as high as a twelve-story building. More terrifying, the Fukushima Daiichi Nuclear Plant experienced a runaway meltdown. There seemed little we could do to help despite the strong desire to do something. Several days later we packed our equipment and headed home.

Japan's main island of Honshu moved eight feet to the east as the Earth shifted almost ten inches off its axis. More than 120,000 buildings collapsed and another million suffered damage during the tsunami. Close to 20,000 people died or went missing and nearly 500,000 evacuated the area.

The Japanese in our neighborhood appeared shaken with understandable fear.

The Air Force planning cell for basic relief efforts, and more importantly for radiation sampling, located their offices in the area where I worked. In addition to providing network connectivity, I supported the special operations contingent with their separate systems. However, the briefing I provided the local neighborhood ranked as the most important thing I did in terms of communications.

Bot filled individual grocery bags with a loaf of bread, a carton of eggs, and a liter of milk. These essentials had emptied from the shelves of local grocery stores. With relief bags in hand, I asked a Japanese-speaking friend to interpret for the neighbors. We gathered along a side street between our houses, and I explained why the base stayed open and active all night long. I related what I knew of the radiological air sampling and assured them that things appeared less dangerous than they imagined. My stature in the neighborhood quietly skyrocketed that afternoon. Far more importantly, the frayed nerves of these wonderful people soothed noticeably. The briefing seemed a small thing at the time, but it turned out to be a much more endearing gesture in the minds of my neighbors.

Chapter 39

Bad things do happen in the world, like war, natural disasters, and disease. But out of those situations always arise stories of ordinary people doing extraordinary things.
– Darny Kagan

ON TUESDAY, JULY 24, 2012, I SHIFTED INTO ultra-slow mode after my right coronary artery completely blocked blood flow.

I'd taken an early lunch and headed for the Par-3 golf course to practice my chronically inconsistent short game. From there I headed home for a shower and to eat a quick lunch before heading back to the office. My wife and daughters had travelled to the Philippines weeks earlier and I found myself alone.

I first felt the blockage while showering and immediately understood the dire situation in which I found myself. I dried off, walked to our tiny living room, and sat on the sofa to gather my thoughts. I'd thrown my clothes in the laundry basket, and only the towel remained. Worse, I'd have to climb a steep set of stairs to get my cell phone and call for help. I found a pair of shorts and pulled them on before coming back down.

Minutes later, six Japanese medics entered the house and loaded me onto a Naugahyde stretcher with six handholds. As my feet approached the door they suddenly dipped as the first two medics slipped into their shoes. They'd removed them, as is the custom when entering a house. Next, my butt dipped precipitously, and finally, my head flopped back. I clung to the sides.

WALK RUN FLY

When I asked for my wallet, the medics crossed their arms in a "no" gesture. They'd secured it in a Ziplock bag and left it on the counter. That's exactly where I found it days later.

Good fortune shined on me that day. Co-worker Bruce Harkness and his Japanese wife, Yatsumi, arrived before the medics could whisk me off to a random hospital. Yatsumi insisted they take me to Tokai University Hospital where she felt they'd provide superior care. I had no idea at the time where I'd been taken.

Two very attractive young nurses approached my gurney in the emergency room holding area. In a soft Japanese tone, they explained they'd need to shave my crotch – something about my femoral artery. Yes!!! This might not be so bad after all! I envisioned Austin Powers in Goldmember chatting with Fook Yu and Fook Mi. At that exact moment, a much older nurse interrupted and announced she'd first insert a urinary catheter. Game over.

The surgeon cleared my arterial blockage and then painlessly inserted a single stent. I craned sideways to watch the wall of monitors bordering the operating table as he completed the procedure. An hour later he rolled me to his replay booth and with great pride, showed a recording of what he'd just accomplished. I already felt better. Someone rolled me along several hallways to a recovery room.

The nursing and surgical staff knew they had a troublesome patient when, after having trouble swallowing rice, I seriously suggested that a shot of whisky would relax my esophageal muscle. They puréed everything thereafter.

My wife arrived from the Philippines, and rather than talk to her at the bedside, I asked her to lie down beside me. Just as we became comfortable, my new chief surgeon entered the room. She set an easy-to-achieve standard for my discharge, and I left for home two days later.

Two days after that I returned to work.

November 2013 brought with it a worsening storm in the Pacific called Haiyan. Within days it reached super typhoon status. Thousands of people in its path evacuated their homes. Then a storm surge of between ten and seventeen feet hit the Philippines provincial capital of Tacloban, whose elevation averaged only ten feet above sea level.

I'd flown to Tacloban City's airport many times in previous years. Its beautiful runway extended into a large horseshoe bay where it became susceptible to storm winds gusting inland from the ocean. One afternoon, the copilot and I, along with several Embassy staff, found ourselves trapped when an approaching typhoon unleashed torrential rains and out-of-limit winds before we could get airborne and fly southward. I secured our small aircraft and hoped for clear morning skies. We'd spend the night in an old colonial hotel feasting on a traditional Philippine fish ceviche dish called kinilaw tanique. San Miguel beer flowed freely. The old Spanish architecture, the fish, the beer, and the torrential rains transported me to earlier times. I felt akin to colonial traders riding out the storm in a bustling seaport.

This central city had been the home of Imelda Marcos, who moved there when eight years old. Immediately south along the coastal road, a large religious shrine dominated the landscape. I noticed an elegant mansion that once held Imelda's infamous shoe collection, a community hall fit for a much larger city, and a large Sto. Nino's Church. We'd visit these another day.

Typhoons hit this area every year. The one we currently watched from Tokyo would be the 24th of the year, but it'd be the most devastating. According to the Joint Typhoon Warning Center, sustained winds lashed out at 195mph with gusts over 235mph. Power lines snapped, roofs separated from storm-proof buildings, winds sucked out building walls, and propelled shards of corrugated steel through the air.

"There aren't many buildings that can withstand that kind of wind," meteorology expert Jeff Masters told the Associated Press of Haiyan's 195-mph landfall. "The wind damage should be the most extreme in Philippines history."

By the night of November 9, the death toll climbed from 138 to more than 1,200 people, and the numbers continued rising sharply.

In the 36th Airlift Squadron, we waited. We prepped our deployment equipment, organized the aircrews, and waited. A week passed and we hadn't been tasked, then ten days. Finally, the word came to immediately send six aircraft.

The seven-hour flight felt like an eternity.

Once on the ground, we wasted little time finding a place to establish operations. The Marine Corps had been in place for nearly a week and provided us with several rooms in a bare-bones contingency building.

"Only in the Philippines ..."

All electrical outlets utilized two prongs because their wiring systems didn't include a common ground. Normally, a person never knew the difference. But our work tables consisted of old metal rectangles that had seen much better days. Electrical current traveled from the wall outlet to our laptop computers and if a metal portion of the computer touched the table, then a low current flowed to the tabletop. Navigators sat at these tables to plan missions, and if they had their sleeves rolled up, they'd get zapped with small electrical shocks. I never could create an acceptable grounding path to eliminate the problem. It became easier to cover the tables with cardboard sheets.

Notes from my journal ...
November 17, 2013.

> Arrived in the Philippines late last night to help with the ongoing disaster relief/humanitarian assistance effort. Another eighteen-hour day getting to the hotel around 2 a.m.

The process by which the aircrews received mission taskings became similarly awkward. The insanity of the system rooted itself in our limited communications. Three geographically separate planning centers needed to share information. The main mission developers resided in Manila. They tracked the available aid and who ultimately needed it. They worked in a bustling, dynamic environment, and our planners remained in periodic contact with them to understand the daily requirements. The problem became more complex with so many different groups available to provide airlift – the Marine Corps flew a couple of KC-130s and six MV-22 tiltrotor Ospreys. The "big" Air Force flew huge C-17 cargo aircraft. Special operations operated several MC-130s, and of course, our six C-130s joined the mix. The tasking of units and aircraft against specific missions occurred in Hawaii where Pacific Command planners did their thing.

WALK RUN FLY

The problem. The Internet remained unreliable and often not available at all. Commercial telephones seldom connected reliably enough for long-distance calls. Even several satellite terminals seemed problematic when trying to connect all the right people. Cellphones worked best … but still, the tasking generally originated in Manila and flowed directly to our planning cell. We'd then call Pacific Command and tell them what missions they should assign to us. Crazy.

Notes from my journal …
November 19, 2013.

> We're flying nights with the Special Ops guys and the Marines have day ops. Providing around-the-clock relief to blacked-out, short airfields. Medical supplies in, evacuees out (120 at a time). They sit on the cargo floor for the one-hour flight to Manila. Planners are tired but keep working long shifts to keep relief flowing.

> … the aircraft commander on our first crew into Tacloban did not have the approval to take evacuees out … she almost cried and still feels heartbroken about leaving some behind in the middle of the night

> … seasoned security teams appeared emotionally spent after transporting the injured out of Tacloban. They couldn't wait to get there and help but hated to see such suffering and devastation. There are a thousand more evacuees at the airport and lots of remote areas awaiting food and water. The relief goes on around the clock with U.S. support.

November 21, 2013.

Lots of injured adults and tired children coming out of Tacloban ... only an occasional backpack, mostly just clothes on their backs. Still flying around the clock delivering relief supplies.

... MC-130 crew picked up one-hundred-plus evacuees the night before last – dark, raining, cold. A husband and wife, each shivering on the metal floor of the aircraft hugging small children to their chests. A contractor and loadmaster took off their jackets to wrap around them for the flight. Every evacuee, everyone, took time to say "thank you" as they left the plane.

... an MC-130 flew into Borongan airfield just north of Tacloban last night in bad weather, offloaded relief supplies, and then evacuated one hundred-plus Filipinos. This struck me as interesting because the runway length extended only 3900' (that's short!) and had trees so close the aircraft couldn't turn around. It backed up the length of the runway for take-off. Bad weather, inky black, no lights within a hundred miles, no navaids, just aircraft instruments to find the field and land. Quiet professionals at work.

Americans, Filipinos, everyone feels pain essentially the same, it's just that some complain a lot less ... talked with the chief special ops physician today and will follow up with details from medics tomorrow ... attendants moved the most seriously injured from provincial hospitals to the airport for transport to Manila, including those with broken femurs, pelvis bones, etc., mostly in wheelchairs – no complaints. Without our airlift and medications, they'd have suffered far worse.

I asked the squadron commander if I could observe first-hand a relief mission to Tacloban and he approved it. I grabbed earplugs and a headset and joined the evening crew. The aircraft commander had recently upgraded from co-pilot. This marked one of the few flights he'd flown since then.

We flew thirty-five minutes from Clark Air Base to Ninoy Aquino International Airport in Manila. A small tarmac for the Philippines' Villamor Air Base existed at the far end of its only international runway. It's where airmen built, organized, and loaded all the relief pallets onto participating aircraft. We loaded our pallets and taxied to the runway.

The tower controller warmed my heart when she expedited our departure. As we taxied for take-off at the far end of the airport, we quickly found ourselves behind ten large commercial airliners. It'd delay our departure by at least thirty minutes. Then the female controller's voice announced.

"Trek 22, can you accept an immediate intersection departure for your disaster relief mission?"

Our aircraft commander hesitated.

"She's trying to expedite our departure," I explained.

In mentioning the disaster relief mission, the controller cleverly informed all the others why she provided such unusual priority. Nice.

As we flew down the center of the country, I couldn't help but notice how few lights illuminated the blackened countryside below. It became clear that the electrical grid remained down.

Our approach and landing at Daniel Z. Romualdez Airport would be without the aid of lights. The aircrew adjusted their night-vision goggles and proceeded to the airport for an uneventful landing.

The airport and its immediate vicinity reside on a small dollop of land surrounded by water on three and a half sides. As the terminal came into view, Haiyan's total devastation overwhelmed us. Only a concrete shell remained. The paint had been scoured clean from the walls. Corrugated panels, trees, and everything other than reinforced concrete became twisted, ripped, and randomly strewn about. I'd never seen such destruction.

As airport helpers and the aircrew downloaded relief supplies, I walked around the ramp and talked with several Filipinos. They stood patiently in a long line hoping for a ride to Manila. Some had been at the airport for days. Kids had peed in place because no facilities existed and they risked losing their place in line if they left it. Most of those in line appeared to be small children. Everyone seemed to be in shock. Normally happy and joking Filipinos stood quiet and tired, hopeful.

Technically, our mission included delivering relief supplies and not providing airlift for survivors. Officially airlifting survivors required time-consuming delays, but doing it on a space-available basis accomplished everyone's goal of providing timely support.

Accordingly, that's precisely what every aircrew did. We loaded 110 people, mostly children, a few adults, and the elderly. One man in a wheelchair boarded last. Everyone sat on the floor, packed as tightly as possible. For most, this represented their first time on an airplane. They should have been excited, but they looked exhausted and fell asleep shortly after takeoff. Family members would meet them at Villamor Air Base in Manila and integrate the children into the local school system.

We felt tired too. Tacloban's middle-of-the-night gloom sucked the energy out of everyone. We started our takeoff roll.

"Abort!" the engineer called.

The pilot retarded the throttles and slowed to taxi speed as we approached the inky end of the runway. The co-pilot hadn't set flaps to fifty percent, and that would have lengthened our required take-off roll a lot. I sat in the rear of the cockpit on the crew bunk, suddenly more awake and alert.

The approach into Manila proceeded normally, that is, until touchdown. Things happened fast.

Approach Control had sequenced eight aircraft a mile apart behind us, all approaching to land. We touched down perfectly. Then, both right tires blew, the wing dipped dangerously low, and the number four propeller whizzed around only feet off the runway.

I clicked the mic button.

"If you can control it, think about exiting via the high-speed turnoff. If we stop on the runway, we'll shut down the airport for the night. It'll be an international incident."

The high-speed turnoff crossed a much shorter runway, so we continued a slow taxi.

"There. That dark ramp is where we should go. If we stop on the parallel taxiway we'll shut down the relief operations because none of the aircraft will be able to get around us."

Despite the uncomfortable taxi, we made it. Next came a ground evacuation into the dark. Kids, adults, and the aircrew exited in an orderly flow and gathered on the ramp. Buses would come to fetch them. Taxiing the aircraft to the ramp area averted so many major issues.

I found the navigator.

"Listen, I'm going to find my way to the Villamor ramp and catch a flight back to Clark. I'll make sure that leadership knows what happened and why you taxied to the ramp. Make sure the aircraft commander knows I'm gone."

I disappeared into the dark and flagged down a service vehicle. A team of Filipino food service workers greeted me as I climbed in beside them. They seemed friendly and curious. The driver stopped as close as he dared to Villamor. I climbed out and walked into the bright lights of the tarmac. Eventually, I crossed in front of an aircraft that had parked with engines running and climbed up to the cockpit. They agreed to take me with them to Clark.

I dressed in civilian clothes the entire time and felt lucky I hadn't been arrested or shot. The aircrew I left behind ultimately won the annual Pacific Air Forces Flight Safety Award for their actions that night.

Notes from my journal …
November 23, 2013.

> Military medics are an interesting/incredible breed … you might form a mental picture of Hawkeye operating in M*A*S*H or a field medic in an old war movie field

dressing a wound. The reality is sometimes a bit different.

Officially, medics can only find, fix, and medicate DoD personnel, and that's officially what they told me. Almost immediately after the two-hundred-mile-per-hour typhoon winds ripped through eastern Samar and Leyte islands, our medics began assisting with medical situations. They cleaned and treated small, deep wounds that would otherwise become infected. They stabilized fractures and loaded many, many survivors on C-130s (sometimes a very painful undertaking) for flights to Manila where they could receive better treatment. Gut-wrenching for sure. These current-day Hawkeyes provided comfort, gave snacks to those being evacuated, and ultimately saved lives. They slept in the open, got soaked at night, and fought off mosquitos like everyone else. These are humble professionals who dwell in the compassionate part of humanity. The need for their urgent care is now transitioned to the care provided by medical teams, NGOs, and of course, the existing medical infrastructure.

It felt like discovering the first green sprout of grass after a huge forest fire ... Late last night from the skies over Samar I spotted quite a few lights, which meant the electrical grid had come back up. Very good news. Many pallets of USAID supplies still awaited delivery to the major airports, but the real challenge continues to be getting the goods from there to the people. Our role of airlifting emergency supplies is fading.

November 27, 2013.

> The immigration agent stamped my passport and said, "Thank you for helping our countrymen;" a security guard offered me a seat out of the sun, and thanked me as I waited for my ride. ... mission complete for me; heading home in the morning but remembering those still struggling to survive.

One interesting off-shoot of all these deployments included occasionally getting a day off. The lull in operations allowed aircrews to adjust flying schedules and allowed maintenance personnel to work on aircraft problems. Those free days allowed me to explore local golf courses. Every outing seemed special. The courses looked beautiful and meticulously maintained, and most required the use of caddies. It provided a different perspective and introduced me to different people. Each outing offered an incredible, fun experience.

Chapter 40

Greatest vacation opportunity ever! I wouldn't miss it for anything.
– SRA Gilbreaith

THE HISTORY OF GOLF TRIPS PROBABLY DATES back to 15th Century Scotland where today's version of the game found its roots. Many years later, the idea of organizing a low-cost exotic golf adventure for young airmen came to mind.

Previous to this, I'd discovered more than thirty high-quality courses within reach of Pattaya, Thailand. On those rare non-flying days during training exercises, I'd spend the day playing golf. The course layouts challenged the best golfers, and their beauty rivaled any others I'd seen. All courses required a caddy. It definitely added to the experience. The associated fees seemed a pittance, less than some municipal courses in the U.S. I'd discovered a hidden gem and felt compelled to share it.

The inaugural golf trip took place in 2007 and included four golfers. Tad supervised air traffic controllers at Yokota Air Base when not golfing; Jeff worked as a Unit Deployment Manager, and sixty-seven-year-old Alan owned a lampshade store in Half Moon Bay, California. We comprised a diverse group, to say the least.

Alan had befriended my brother years earlier and joined us based on a good-faith recommendation. His affliction with cerebral palsy never impeded his play, although putting with recognizable control presented a challenge. In an attempt to solve the problem, he'd filled his putter shaft with lead. The darned thing weighed almost twenty pounds but seemed impervious to his twitches. Alan joked non-stop between golf shots and initiated a ritual of proposing to his female caddies on the first tee box of each round. Normally shy caddies glowed inwardly. It provided a glimpse of how much fun they'd have during our round. Alan fit in quite well.

We played a different course on each of eight consecutive days that first year. On the seventh day, we played two courses. In the second year, eight golfers played two courses each day. To make it work, a few of us scheduled wake-up calls at 5 a.m. Several others returned from the bars around that time. I always scheduled our first tee time at 6:30 a.m. We'd be the first groups to tee off as no one else in Thailand did much of anything that early. We finished playing shortly before sunset, had a few drinks, ate, and then went to bed or went elsewhere. This felt like golfer's heaven … or perhaps, insanity.

By Golf Trip 11, a dozen players from around the world – United States, Japan, Philippines, India, and Korea converged on Pattaya. We returned to playing a single course each day and even set aside Saturday for doing touristy things. After so many years, less felt better.

I considered various lodging alternatives each year and we relocated when it suited our needs. I reserved rooms at the

Hog's Breath Hotel based on the recommendation of some Navy Seals who preferred its low-visibility, low-cost arrangement. But we struggled with hauling our golf clubs up and down the narrow stairways, something that wouldn't have phased the Seals. The next day we moved to Lewinski's Golf Bar and Restaurant. Lewinski's served alcohol but it functioned more as a restaurant and gathering place for local golfers. I loved the rich atmosphere where crusty old golfers gathered to argue the Rules of Golf over a beer or three. Although quite close to Pattaya's infamous Walking Street, it remained delightfully isolated from much of the associated noise.

Our half of the block consisted of quiet bars and restaurants along with two tailor shops. The other half hosted gay and transsexual bars. Al recommended getting a haircut at a gay barbershop that separated Lewinski's from the Blue Bar district. Several of us took his suggestion and enjoyed the experience.

In later years, we moved to the more relaxed Sabai Resort on the northern side of town. It featured several beautiful swimming pools and vastly better rooms. More importantly, its location kept us from the daily traffic snarls we endured closer to Walking Street.

Pattaya brings thoughts of a vivid nightlife to many. Thousands of bars share the landscape with high-rise hotels, shopping bazaars, and great ethnic restaurants. After a bit of online research and soliciting the aircrews for preferred restaurants, I created a dining schedule ... it seemed promising.

One night I paid the van drivers overtime and asked if they'd drive us to Mum-Aroi, a non-touristy seafood restaurant that perched on moorings above the ocean.

Boiled crabs, grilled fish, spicy vegetables, and a variety of soups soon filled our table. Beer flowed amid lively conversations.

We ordered fresh calzone and drank German beers from giant frosted mugs at the Hopf Brauhaus. Sue's Bar had long been a favorite for the aircrew. Ironically, her place existed only half a block away from Lewinski's. One wall displayed fifty or more pictures of grouped aircrew. A few additional photos showed some rather unique characters. I recognized one of them, an ultra-light student from several years earlier. I discovered that he'd married Sue's daughter. I lived in a small world. Sue's looked nothing like a Mexican restaurant but it did offer excellent Mexican cuisine. We even tried a place called Cabbage and Condom. They donated a portion of their profits to some birth control foundation. The food didn't strike any of us as special. Weird place. We never returned.

From the Sabai Resort Hotel, we walked a short distance to Jameson's Bar. It became a favorite spot for our last group dinner on each trip. Televised rugby games entertained the more impassioned Aussi and British regulars. Unfortunately, they shuttered their doors for good during the Covid-19 pandemic.

Odd things always seemed to pop up. One year Roland hadn't paid attention to the airline weight restrictions and arrived at the check-in counter with quite a bit of excess – four hundred dollars of excess to be exact.

One of our younger Yokota Air Base golfers packed all his things the morning of his flight and arrived at the airport without his passport. Narita International Airport is sixty miles from the Air Base and filled with congested metro-

Tokyo between the two. He eventually caught an evening fight and although tired, made every tee time.

More than forty different golfers joined the trips over the years. Jeff, Big Al, Mex, Moses, Gary "Frog Hair", Nori, Jose, Roland, Randy, and Big Bill all hold special memories.

Years earlier Nardo brought his wife for the first few days. It turned out to be a great idea and certainly didn't diminish the activities of anyone else. Al and I decided to bring our wives several years later, and while we golfed they toured several attractions. On the non-golfing day, Bot and I visited the Sanctuary of Truth, a jaw-dropping carved wooden temple. A large crew of woodcarvers had already chiseled away for thirty-nine years and planned to continue for another five. The scale of the project and the size of the structure took my breath away. We then attended a crocodile exhibition, an elephant demonstration, and a wild tiger show. We came away with mixed emotions. I looked forward to getting back on the golf course.

A similar golf trip came together for the Philippines. We played five different courses and decided to expand the venue in the upcoming years.

During the summer months preceding the trips, excitement always grew, players practiced more, and visions of perfect shots on breathtaking fairways filled our minds.

My underlying motivation for coordinating so many loose ends centered on providing an affordable cultural experience for young airmen who wanted to do more than lay on a beach or sit in a bar. I brought together individuals who otherwise never would have crossed paths. They shared different perspectives on golf, socializing, and life. Age didn't matter. We ran the gamut from eighteen to seventy. One's ethnicity never entered our minds. We identified as golfers and that's all that mattered.

Chapter 41

Business opportunities are like buses, there's always another one coming.
– Richard Branson

"Now, that's an odd email…"

I MUSED TO MYSELF AFTER READING AN unexpected message from Joel Tubig. I'd taught him to fly sports planes years earlier and we remained friends. He inquired about how to inspect a used helicopter for general airworthiness.

What the heck? Did he intend to buy a helicopter?

"Well, you might open the cowling and see if there are spider webs. Are there hydraulic or oil leaks? Is everything connected … no obvious missing parts."

I hit the send key and thought that would be the last of it.

"How much is a used Gazelle worth?" Joel asked.

I knew a Gazelle helicopter had one engine but not much more. After a bit of research, I learned that many countries flew them, primarily France and the United Kingdom. Its design originated with Sud Aviation and Aerospatiale, and Westland Aircraft later produced them. I gave Joel several very general value estimates depending on whether it could be flown or if it amounted to little more than an accumulation of parts.

Joel used those estimates to win a UK Ministry of Defense liquidation auction for thirty Gazelles. Several weeks later, my wife and I joined Joel and his wife in Hong

Kong and flew from there to London. I inspected his Gazelles even though I felt marginally qualified to assess their true value. I'd guessed right on the original cost estimate, and my initial assessment that perhaps sixteen of the thirty could be economically renovated matched a similar valuation by mechanics who knew helicopters better than me. Joel tracked down and contacted a French helicopter expert by the name of Philippe Thenaisie.

We met outside a classy restaurant near King's Cross. It felt extremely James Bond-ish. We formed a three-way partnership to sell a squadron of renovated Gazelles to the Philippine Air Force. Joel would finalize an unsolicited proposal and the sale of the aircraft. Philippe would manage a workforce to disassemble the helicopters, crate them for shipment, and then reassemble and test-fly them once delivered to the Philippines. I'd develop a business plan, organize all the details, and determine overall costs. I'd also find a way to get some stick time in the process.

I worked sleepless nights and weekends when not supporting Air Force flight mission planning. I also managed the issue of having a security clearance and owning a foreign aerospace company at the same time. I traveled to Manila more than a few times during the next months. Joel, Philippe and I briefed Commanding Generals at the Philippine Air Force and Army, Admirals at the Philippine Navy and Coast Guard, and the Philippine Secretary of Defense.

One Friday after work I caught a flight from Tokyo to Manila for a weekend meeting. I'd be home on Sunday night, or so I thought ... the Immigration Officer asked some unusual questions about my having had an Investor Visa in the past.

"Yes, I had one almost fifteen years ago."

Another agent then asked me to follow him to the office. After further explanations about my not having filed a required report fifteen years earlier, they deported me the following morning.

Oh brother, unbelievable. How do these things happen to me?

A guard stayed with me all night. I mostly sat in a plastic departure area chair, but he came along when I visited the restroom. Eight hours later I boarded a Delta Airlines flight back to Tokyo.

As it turned out, the Philippine regulation regarding Investor Visas had changed two years after mine expired. I hadn't complied with the updated guidance and fortunately, hadn't committed a foul. The fact that I never used the visa didn't seem to strengthen my case. I'd entered and exited the country using a diplomatic passport during the entire time frame in question. Technically, I had immunity. Eventually, the government removed my name from their "bad boy" list.

The Gazelle deal eventually fell through when Joel's financial backer wanted too big a cut of the pie. Philippe and I threw up our hands in disgust. I vowed to never sell helicopters to any government unless I could work a government-to-government contract. The corruption and its associated risks remained too high. The aircraft eventually found their way to South Africa with an Israeli company getting the support contract. Philippe and I looked at commercial airplane and helicopter sales and formed our own Philippine company called Vertical Airlift Solutions.

It'd be the prime contractor and my company, Grey Hawk Aviation, would subcontract with them.

U.S.-based Grey Hawk Aviation and Philippine-incorporated Vertical Airlift Solutions logos.

I researched all sorts of aviation opportunities and drafted feasibility studies for those holding promise. My analysis of a proposed company called Bangkok Helicopter VIP Service held great promise. Bangkok's transportation improvements would not match projected growth for the foreseeable future. Existing providers appeared to be fragmented and minimally partnered with commercial airlines. Unfortunately, we struggled to find investors after our key marketing point-man moved to Australia. Crickets.

Philippine off-shore oil exploration required a variety of vertical lift, from shuttling oil rig workers to providing shipboard support. Within weeks of finalizing that rather optimistic study, an Australian helicopter company landed a large support contract. My report began collecting dust.

I looked at Visayas regional helicopter operations based out of Mactan Island in Cebu, Philippines. Under this scheme, a small fleet of helicopters time-shared operations with resort hotels, missionary services, and supported inter-island and Manila medivac flights. More dust.

A friend named Wik told me of several businessmen in Koh Samui, Thailand, who'd expressed interest in starting a helicopter business catering to tourists. After numerous exploratory conversations, Wik, Philippe, and I flew to Thailand, assessed their specific needs, and submitted a proposal for their review. During the four-day trip, I gathered technical information, analyzed the market, and defined wide-ranging support requirements. I also toured Koh Samui, explored nearby islands, and ate spicy-hot Thai food. In the end, the investors realized their dream represented a reach too far. Too bad. I'd hoped to become their chief pilot.

Short-haul cargo operations also held promise. I worked with the President of Basler Turbo out of Oshkosh, Wisconsin, in determining configurations for turbo-powered DC-3s for Thailand and Vietnam. These aircraft offered somewhat unique capabilities and remained in service around the globe. While I never marketed these aircraft directly, I did analyze their use.

On a separate initiative, I developed a business plan for quad-copter and unmanned aerial vehicle software development. This would be a Philippine initiative, staffed by local college graduates and funded by senior business executives from the United States. When our university recruiter suffered a fatal heart attack and the key Silicon Valley investor retired, the program faded.

Philippe and I eventually set our business pursuits aside and returned to other things. We've kept a close friendship ever since.

Chapter 42

I always wonder why birds stay in the same place when they can fly anywhere on the earth. Then I ask myself the same question.
– Harun Yahya

SOMEWHERE ALONG THE LINE, BOT AND I returned to Colorado Springs and sold what we once thought would be our retirement home. We committed to living in the Philippines and packed the important stuff into a forty-foot shipping container. We could have donated most of the furniture and clothes to St. Vincent DePaul or Goodwill but decided to give much of it directly to needy Filipinos.

Renters let cats, unauthorized cats, pee on our wall-to-wall carpeting. They smashed at least one hole in a wall and let all the normal things deteriorate. At a minimum, the house needed new flooring, cabinets, and countertops before going on the market. What a headache, literally. Thank goodness we found a private contractor who provided a good estimate. By good, I don't mean inexpensive. I reasoned that we could sell the house six months faster with a major makeover. Of course, this all needed a master plan.

Immediately before the renovation, shippers packed everything, took it to Denver for short-term storage, and after several months moved it to the West Coast via train where it'd be trans-loaded to a ship. Once the renovations concluded, our realtor took over. Bot and I returned to Japan.

My Yamaha Roadstar Silverado 1600c.c. motorcycle with only five thousand miles would also be shipped but with special considerations. In an attempt to beat prohibitively high Philippine duties and taxes, I planned to send the engine and transmission as individual parts and do the same with the frame.

Apex Sports answered my call from Tokyo.

"Can you pick up the motorcycle from my house, take it to your shop, and do a complete refurbishment? When you get it working to your satisfaction can you then remove the engine and transmission and return everything to the house?"

Their answer, "No."

After discussing it further, they agreed and did a wonderful job. I'm sure they're still scratching their heads even though I've since sent pictures of the Yamaha completely reassembled and displaying Philippine license plates.

I still paid a lot of duty when it arrived.

Our house construction in the Philippines progressed slowly. Too slow. When the shipping container from Colorado arrived we had no place to store its contents ... until the house across the street from the one we currently rented became available. We leased it for six months and loaded everything inside. A nephew slept there along with our large black Labrador.

Building a house in the Philippines, regardless of the contractor or the size of the house, brings certain frustrations. We discovered that our architect had never been certified, had not obtained building permits, and lacked an understanding of quality work. We fired him and found a legitimate contractor who resolved all of the major issues. Toward the end, we farmed out a lot of specialty work. The cost increased slightly but quality soared and things got done. Some days we'd have four or five construction teams working on various projects. We always fed them lunch and as a result, received a fair day's effort.

One last item needed resolution. It involved shipping my pet cockatoo, Sammy, to the Philippines.

Sammy hatched thirteen years earlier in New Jersey. I bought him from a reputable breeder who put him on a Continental Airlines flight to Denver, and we drove up from Colorado Springs to get him. Importing him into Japan in 1990 turned out to be easier than importing our pet dog. Unfortunately, avian influenza spread throughout Asia several years later, and shipping exotic birds became more difficult. The Philippines wouldn't accept exotic birds from Japan. Period.

This required more thought. I dug deeper and realized that I could, however, ship a cockatoo from the U.S. After all, that's where Sammy originated. I'd simply state that Sammy originated in the U.S. and had a connecting flight in Japan. The twelve-year flight connection delay didn't need to be highlighted. I obtained an export permit from the U.S. and used it to process the import permit from the Philippines. Somehow, I assembled the required supporting documentation and received a Philippine import permit. Quarantine clearance became more important than the import permit and miraculously, Bot successfully coordinated that clearance. We seemed to be all set and only needed to find an airline that accepted pets. Not one would take the bird.

Maybe, just maybe, if a C-130 from Yokota Air Base flew to the Philippines and if I could find legitimate work to do there, then I could ride along without having to process the bird via normal procedures. I suspected that passenger terminal airmen wouldn't authorize a bird on this or any other military flight, but I'd find a way…

A potential aerial-delivery drop zone near Clark Air Base needed to be surveyed and I possessed the requisite qualification to do just that. It justified a flight status that bypassed the passenger terminal. When the aircraft commander on the flight changed from our shop chief to the Operational Support Squadron Commander, my scheme faced another obstacle. I'd have to explain the part about carrying a bird onboard. The explanation didn't go exactly as I'd hoped.

"Sir, I need to explain something about your flight to the Philippines. I'll be bringing a cockatoo along. I assure you, it's all legal and I have all the necessary paperwork."

"Terry, that's not the way C-130s do business," he explained.

"That's how they've done business since the beginning of time," I countered. "They've hauled pigs and goats. I've heard of them carrying elephants. This is nothing compared to any of that."

He smiled.

"I'll need to see all the paperwork before we go."

"Yes sir."

Of course, he didn't need to see anything too soon. That'd only give him time to find a reason to deny Sammy a seat. I'd give him a copy of the paperwork an hour before take-off.

I carried Sammy directly from the flying squadron to the aircraft in an insulated gym bag. The flight departed four hours late and due to strong headwinds lasted seven hours. Sammy seemed unfazed by the long flight or the cold temperatures. Bot had flown to the Philippines and met me at the edge of the tarmac. She took Sammy while I cleared immigration without the bird. Sammy would undergo processing the next day at our ultimate destination. He rode as cargo in an Airbus A-320 cargo hold to the central Philippines. This entire episode transpired within the limits of "legal" even though it rarely felt that way.

We shipped a smaller container from Tokyo to the Philippines a couple of months later and boarded a one-way flight to our new home.

Sammy loved the Philippines for a year after his arrival. It broke my heart when he suddenly died of natural causes.

Life settled into a pleasant routine. The slower pace and beautiful surroundings relaxed us. We explored the mountains and swam in hot springs. Mt Kanlaon's molten core just seventeen miles to our east kept the waters hot. We bought a hundred acres of fish ponds, hired several workers, and began a fish-farming business. I'd toyed with the idea of writing a novel since well before retirement but held off until our move to the Philippines. I'd settled into a manageable routine. It seemed like a good time to start writing.

I wrote about an adventure in Thailand. Characters came alive as I lay in bed and dreamed snippet after snippet of an evolving storyline. I spiced the narrative with Thai culture and recreated the smells, the taste, and the sounds of rural life. An initial draft existed after three months and the process of editing began. Hours upon hours of adjustment opened my eyes to the need for refinement, consistency, and proper grammar. Before the book found its way to online outlets, major adjustments took place. The preface and prologue disappeared. The first chapter changed completely. When my editor, Barbara, stepped in, I realized just how amateurish my style had been. She provided blunt, honest, encouraging, and sharp advice. I curled her toes more than once with mind-numbing introductory phrases and overuse of time references. She opened my eyes to more effective sentence structure and how to make the text flow. The book felt complete. I decided to write another.

In book two, Philippine culture, terminology, and background settings took center stage. The story evolved and I challenged myself to add historical twists in weaving a tale of intrigue. I'd developed a writing process that seemed to work. It involved developing a broad outline for the entire story. Chapter by chapter, the detail of the outline expanded. My writing flowed with direction and I kept close to the planned storyline. The initial draft of each chapter lacked detail, effective word selection, and simple sentence structure. Multiple rewrites added flavor and defined the narrative like a sculptor chiseling his statue.

Book number three built on techniques learned during the preceding months. I added more romance and lessened background dumps. Writing in an active voice became more natural. Expressing feelings became more "show" and less "tell."

The whole process generated mental activity. It wore me out at times and stimulated endorphins at others. It never matched flying, but it proved to be pretty darn rewarding.

I've written six novels and have just completed rewriting each of them. Novel number seven remains in the formative stage, but will soon begin moving from my head to the computer.

Chapter 43

The secret of a good sermon is to have a good beginning and a good ending, then have the two as close together as possible.
– George Burns

I'D HIT MY STRIDE. WARM, FRESH MORNING AIR ceded to sticky afternoon warmth. In my dreams, I flew to interesting places, squeezed a Carbon Cub aircraft between jungle trees, and landed on a mud-caked road, or dodged building mountain storms to rescue lost hikers. Between writing books, exploring the central mountains and coastal shorelines, fish farming, and dreaming, Philippine retirement felt good.

But then an ounce of restlessness crept in. A feeling of freedom whispered, "Live your dreams."

I'd been researching an Indonesian airline that landed at precarious jungle and mountain-top airstrips. Susi Air came to life in 2004 following the Indonesian tsunami that had wreaked havoc on Sumatra. At the time, Christian von Strombeck and his wife, Susi Pudjiastuti, possessed two Cessna Grand Caravan C-208Bs and became the only company to donate its aircraft to the government for disaster relief flights. Susi Air grew and filled a niche market hauling people and cargo to and from remote islands and mountain airstrips. Government subsidies infused the necessary revenue to fuel its growth. Rather than hire more expensive experienced flyers, Susi Air employed low-time pilots who happily traded away civilized locations for the opportunity to build hours. I viewed this as a great opportunity to teach and to fly. I applied.

Their response came quickly and sounded enthusiastic … Unfortunately, they insisted that I obtain an FAA single-engine rating. That'd require me to return to the United States, get a place to stay, attend ground school, and then log all the required flight time in a single-engine aircraft. It seemed an unrealistic requirement when I'd fly for them using an Indonesian rating. Plus, I already possessed much more difficult ratings. The limited time that I'd fly didn't justify the time and expense required to obtain the rating.

Undeterred by such a minor detail, I applied with a group called the Missionary Aviation Fellowship. They flew C-208Bs throughout Papua New Guinea. The main drawback included the requirement to become a missionary. Not likely. While I held religious beliefs, I could never become a true evangelistic missionary-type person. Nonetheless, I considered becoming a pseudo-missionary if it meant that I could fly.

I promptly received an email from their hiring manager and we had a great conversation until he realized I'd logged time before he'd been born. My dream of flying for hire had come to an end.

A Facebook post caught my attention several weeks later. It mentioned a new support position for the 353rd Special Operations Group in Okinawa. This would reunite me with special operations, and I'd rub shoulders with a great group of flyers. Bot and I talked. It'd be a temporary change and it'd bring us back to Japan for as long as we liked.

Another reason for moving lurked in the back of my mind. Bot needed open-heart surgery and the best location for the operation and her subsequent recovery seemed to be Tokyo.

We'd need a special visa and taking a job in Japan would solve that.

After a year in Okinawa, I moved to Tokyo and began working for the 21st Special Operations Squadron. Their pilots flew CV-22B tilt-rotor Ospreys, a relatively new and unusual aircraft. I'd flown helicopters alongside the 21st SOS during my time at Nakom Phanom Air Base in Thailand. Joining this unit now brought me full circle.

When I moved to Okinawa, Bot moved to Tokyo. Angelica already lived and worked in the heart of the city where she'd landed a great job several blocks from Tokyo Station. Marie continued with remote college classes and that allowed her to accompany Bot to Tokyo. We became a complete family once again.

Bot delayed the surgery for several months until after our 25th wedding anniversary, which we planned to celebrate back in the Philippines. Then Covid-19 struck. Travel became more and more restrictive and Bot's condition worsened. Several days before Christmas and almost a year later than planned, she walked into the operating room and underwent six hours of surgery. Most Japanese considered her surgeon to be the best in Japan as he'd operated on the Emperor a year earlier.

Following Bot's surgery and full recovery, we remained in Japan until feeling the urge to return to the Philippines. So many wonderful celebrations awaited us there.

Together, we'd found a new lease on life.

As Bot recovered, book number four moved from the back burner to the front. Bot and our two daughters continued pestering me about writing an autobiography. Curiosity about much of my life surfaced here and there, but for them, the first forty years remained a complete mystery. Yet, writing memoirs didn't interest me in the least. I felt uncomfortable recalling a lifetime of good and bad memories and then putting them into some semblance of perspective.

I'd reached a decision point. Either I'd write the darned thing or I'd convince myself not to do it. I felt like I'd voluntarily walked to the end of the immunization line and waited to be stabbed. I'd write my story ... at least most of it.

My days continue to be action-packed. The 21st SOS is young, filled with deceptively intelligent aviators who fly highly technical aircraft in the dark of night. They're as comfortable talking about sports or gardening as they are discussing international relations or physics. I feel like a grandfather watching my grandchildren succeed in a tough, competitive environment.

I sat in on a Navy Seals mission briefing and hoped they didn't hear my bones creaking as I walked into the secure vault. The environment, the work, and the people keep me feeling young. That's a good thing because there's still an awful lot to do.

I recently partnered with Philippe on another business venture. We reached out to a financially strapped Indonesian airline with a proposal to buy and sell their entire aircraft fleet. We're awaiting their response ... The fish ponds are capable of producing more than just fish. I'm analyzing the risk of simultaneously growing prawns. A similar, but separate initiative involves growing higher-value sea bass. Bot and I are considering expanding into more traditional crop farming. We already manage a dozen or so goats.

I'd been lucky to have had a mother and father who took an interest in everything I did. They pointed me toward lofty goals, helped me find ways to achieve them, supported me when appropriate, and let me struggle to better appreciate the consequences of my efforts. In the process, I developed a spiritual sense that required faith in self as well as faith in a greater being. Carefree days of wandering along endless farm trails evolved into disciplined time-study management and targeted goal-setting. Mom and Dad taught me proper ethical and moral standards from an early age. The Air Force provided further definitions and reinforced the same standards of excellence. Life could never have been a successful singular journey. Along the way, I built meaningful relationships. I stumbled and fell more than once, but always found an extended hand to raise me back onto my feet. I committed to hard work, finding fun and adventure in life, and most importantly, loving my family. I should define my family to include not only my sister and brother and Bot and my two daughters, but also the pilots, navigators, engineers, loadmasters, and all the others at the tip-of-the-spear. It's a big family.

The following tenets have brought great satisfaction to my life while guiding me along the way:

1. Be humble
2. Be happy for others' success
3. Be positive
4. Do my best. Accept the result, and

5. Know that others aren't intentionally stupid

The future looks bright. There's still a lot to experience. Looking forward always brings more excitement than looking to the past.

Author Notes

Thank you for reading this adventurous tale and experiencing a few of my wandering recollections. As an author who writes and self-publishes, I very much value your readership. Even more deeply appreciated is your reaction to the book.

Whether you found my words to be gold-encrusted nuggets of brilliance or belabored wanderings fit for the dung heap, I'll never know without your feedback. Potential readers will find your unbiased comments helpful in their purchase decisions. Please leave an Amazon rating, or better yet, a written reaction to what you've read. Feedback is the lifeblood of a good author and the best insight for potential readers.

Please consider reading one of my other novels. Thanks again!